Guests of My Life

Elizabeth
Watson

Guests
of My
Life

Illustrations by Ann Mikolowski

Celo Press

First Printing 1979
Second Printing 1979
Third Printing 1983
Fourth Printing 1986

Published by Celo Press
the printing and publishing department of the
Arthur Morgan School
1901 Hannah Branch Road
Burnsville, NC 28714

ISBN 0-914064-13-4
Library of Congress Catalog Card No. 79-52445

For Jean, John, and Carol
who also lived this story
and who also made their
own special contributions
to my healing

TABLE OF CONTENTS

FOREWORD

This is the story of my personal pilgrimage through grief for a daughter lost in an automobile accident. At each stage of my journey there was a writer whose insights I needed, and when I had worked my way through that period of grief, another writer came forward to help with the next part of the journey. Each of these authors had written of someone who died young. They helped me see that my personal tragedy was part of the universal human experience, so that I could move through it and beyond it. These writers became part of my life — *guests of my life*, in Tagore's phrase. I want to share not only my own story, but something of their seeking, their writing, and my response to their lives and insights.

This book began as a series of lectures given in June 1973 at Friends General Conference, a Quaker gathering held that year at Earlham College, in Richmond, Indiana. I had been asked to speak on "writers who had influenced my spiritual growth," and I kept my personal story to a minimum. The lectures were given again in 1975 at the Earlham School of Religion, and in the spring of 1978 at Pendle Hill, a

Quaker study center in Wallingford, Pennsylvania. And for the last six years, my writers have been shared on Sunday evenings around the fireplace of our home with each entering class at Friends World College in Huntington, New York. Each time the lectures have been given the material has been revised and rewritten, as my understanding of and response to these writers have grown.

I find that my writers have been "guests" in other lives as well as mine. Each time I have shared the material people have responded with illuminating comments, enlarging my own understanding. It is not possible here to mention all those to whom I am indebted for helpful suggestions, but six people need to be acknowledged.

Julia Abrahamson and Jenifer Morgan, both of the Celo Community near Burnsville, North Carolina, read the manuscript with critical eyes. Their penetrating comments have resulted in some revision. I am grateful for their careful and thoughtful consideration of the total work and how the parts fitted together.

Special thanks go to Ann Mikolowski for her sensitive and beautiful illustrations. It was truly a labor of love.

Three people have had central roles in this undertaking. My husband, George Watson, and I have spent many long evenings by the fireplace imagining first the lectures and later the book. We have read and reread aloud what the writers wrote, sharing the ideas, puzzling over passages, and winnowing the material. In addition, every page of every draft has benefitted from George's blue pencil. Whatever may be right and good about this book is in large measure due to his involvement in it.

James and Ann Lenhart who manage Celo Press at the Arthur Morgan School near Burnsville, North Carolina, also have been deeply involved. Jim heard the lectures in 1973 and it was his idea that I should write the book. Both Jim and Ann have read the manuscript at various stages. Their belief in the worth of the material has pulled me through periods of self-doubt and has driven me back to the typewriter. Their comments have always been helpful, their editorial knowledge and skill invaluable, and their enthusiasm contagious. It has been a joy to work with them in the final preparation of the book.

To George, to Ann and Jim, as well as to many other friends, my thanks and my love.

Elizabeth Watson
Huntington, New York
November 1978

ACKNOWLEDGMENTS

Grateful acknowledgment is made to the following publishers and individuals for permission to reprint copyrighted material from the books listed below:

Permission to use the phrase "Guests of My Life" as the title of my book and to reprint poem #75 in CROSSING by Rabindranath Tagore has been granted by Sanat Kumar Bagchi, Curator, Rabindra Bhavana, Santiniketan, West Bengal, India.

Poems from THE COMPLETE POEMS OF EMILY DICKINSON, edited by Thomas H. Johnson, Boston, Mass.: Little, Brown and Company. Copyright 1914, 1942 by Martha Dickinson Bianchi. Copyright 1929 by Martha Dickinson Bianchi. Copyright © 1957 by Mary L. Hampson. Copyright 1935 by Martha Dickinson Bianchi. Copyright © 1963 by Mary L. Hampson.

Poems #633, #657, #789, #943 reprinted by permission of the publishers and the Trustees of Amherst College from THE POEMS OF EMILY DICKINSON, edited by Thomas H. Johnson, Cambridge, Mass.: The Belknap Press of Harvard University Press. Copyright © 1951, 1955 by the President and Fellows of Harvard College.

Material from THE LIFE AND LETTERS OF EMILY DICKINSON by Martha Dickinson Bianchi. Copyright 1924 by Martha Dickinson Bianchi and renewed 1952 by Alfred Leete Hampson. Reprinted by permission of Houghton Mifflin Company.

Poems from POEMS 1906-1926 and LATER POEMS, by Rainer Maria Rilke, translated by J.B. Leishman, used by permission of St. John's College, Oxford, and The Hogarth Press Ltd., London.

Material from DUINO ELEGIES by Rainer Maria Rilke, translated by J.B. Leishman and Stephen Spender, used with permission of W.W. Norton & Company, Inc., Copyright 1939 by W.W. Norton & Company, Inc. Copyright renewed 1967 by Stephen Spender and J.B. Leishman. Permission also granted

Sara at Antioch College

GUESTS OF MY LIFE

You came in the early dawn, and you in the night.

Your name was uttered by the Spring flowers, and yours by the showers of rain.

You brought the harp into my house and you brought the lamp.

After you had taken your leave I found God's footprints on my floor.

Now when I am at the end of my pilgrimage I leave in the evening flowers of worship my salutations to you all.

—*Rabindranath Tagore*

PROLOGUE

Friday afternoon, June 5, 1964, was warm and lovely as we headed east from our home in Chicago — George and I, my mother, and our three daughters. We were driving to Radnor Friends Meeting, outside Philadelphia, to attend our son's wedding. Carol and Jean had returned earlier in the week from school in Iowa — Carol having finished her freshman year at Scattergood School, and Jean her junior year at Grinnel College. Sara was living at home that year, taking graduate work at the University of Chicago. My mother had come from La Jolla, California, to go with us to the wedding of her only grandson. It was a long time since we had all been together, and it was a happy journey. We enjoyed a picnic supper and late in the evening we stopped for the night at a motel near Pittsburgh. The girls tried on their dresses and Sara finished hemming the one she had made to wear at the wedding.

The wedding the next day was simple and beautiful. Phyllis, our son's bride, wore her grandmother's wedding gown, with lace from her great grandmother's dress. She carried wild flowers and she looked supremely happy. After the manner of Friends, there was no minister, but a meeting for worship based on silence, lasting for about an hour. John and Phyllis exchanged their vows without prompting, and afterwards many Friends spoke out of the silence, wishing them well and giving them their blessing.

In the evening the two families gathered for dinner. We had not met Phyllis's family before this day. We liked them, finding we had many things in common—shared values and shared hopes for our two young people. The memory of that beautiful day is still fresh and vivid.

We retired early, for we needed to be on the road the first thing the next morning, to make the trip all in one day. We shared the driving. After two lovely days, the weather suddenly had turned very hot, and both the people and the car needed to be cooled and rested from time to time. Although we stopped frequently, we made good time. Late in the afternoon we were approaching the western border of Ohio when someone remarked that we should make it home between 9 and 10.

And then the tire blew and the car went out of control.

Hours later the kindly doctor at the small town hospital sat down by my bed to discuss the family. George's head had literally held up the car roof. The severity of his concussion meant his life hung in the balance. If he survived the night, he might make it, the doctor said. His orthopedic injuries would have to wait. My mother too had a severe concussion and multiple injuries. She was to spend much of the remaining eleven years of her life in hospitals, although we could not see the length of her ordeal at the time. Jean's shoulder was broken and Carol had two cracked vertebrae. The hospital was not equipped to take care of them. I had internal injuries, but no broken bones.

But Sara was dead.

She was our first-born, named for the poet, Sara Teasdale. She was twenty-three that summer of 1964. She had just completed her second year of work toward a doctorate in human development. Early in life she had found her calling. She came home from school one day when she was about eight, with shining eyes. "Mommie," she said, "I know what I want to be when I grow up. I'm going to be a teacher." She was blessed that year with an unusually gifted and perceptive teacher, but Sara's calling persisted even in years when she had teachers with no vocation for their task.

In high school she had a friend with cerebral palsy. Sara learned how specially trained teachers had helped this girl learn to speak and to overcome her handicap in many ways. Sara knew then that she wanted to teach handicapped children. She chose to go to Antioch College so that she might use the work periods to explore different handicaps and different ways of working with children. In her junior year she worked at the Children's Guild, a center for emotionally disturbed children in Baltimore. She knew then that she had finally found her precise calling. She went back for a second quarter. (The Children's Guild named their library in her honor, after they learned of her death.) After college she began her professional training, expecting to earn not only a doctorate, but certification as a clinical psychologist.

She also was taking two private voice lessons a week. It almost seemed that she was born singing. By the time she was three she could carry a tune accurately, picking up quickly songs she heard on the radio or record player. In kindergarten her room performed for a school assembly. Our Sara stepped forth from the ranks to sing the verses of the song — with confidence, with clear diction, and right on pitch, her classmates joining her on the choruses. In eighth grade she was chosen to sing with an all-Chicago school chorus. She sang with the choral groups at Antioch College. For years she had wanted to study voice, and when back in Chicago for graduate work she found the right teacher to help her. The score of *La Traviata* lay on her lap as we travelled.

We had always been close. As I thought about her before she was born, the gift I wanted most for her was freedom to be herself. As it turned out, she was very like me in reactions, likes and dislikes, thought and speech habits. Discipline was never a problem. I always understood how she felt and could explain things so that she understood and cooperated. It was not always easy to see her as a separate individual to whom the freedom to be had been promised as I had anticipated. In so many ways she seemed like part of myself—a stronger, better, more competent part.

When she was four, and Jean and John not much more than a year old, George was drafted. Conscientious objectors in the Second World War received neither pay nor dependents' allotments. He was sent to a forestry camp near Elmira, New York. The children and I moved to a settlement house in Chicago where I worked to support us, with our slender savings as a backlog for emergencies. The younger children went to an excellently run, federally financed day nursery affiliated with the settlement. Sara entered kindergarten that year and was part of play groups at the house.

With George gone, I often turned to Sara, four-going-on-five, to talk about many things. She rose to this responsibility in a remarkable degree. She took on not only sharing of easy companionship and concern for the younger children, but also the task of trying to keep up my morale. All her life I turned to her for friendship, for comfort, for advice.

What are the limits of protection of a child for whom you have wished the gift of freedom? Where do you draw the line between letting a child go forth as she may feel led, and protecting her from situations you judge possibly dangerous to body, or mind, or spirit? Can you stand in the way of her accepting the adventures that come to her, if you truly give her freedom to be herself? I often wrestled with these questions.

I learned that ultimately we cannot protect our children from hardships, disease, accidents, encounters with evil, even death. The best we can hope to do is to help them learn to take care of themselves, to accept responsibility for their actions, to care about other people, and to acquire ''coping skills'' through experience.

To this end, I am glad we chose the city—Chicago—with all its violence, dirt, sordidness, and danger—but also its opportunities for learning, its sheer excitement, its neighborliness, and its variety of people—as the place for our family to live. And our children are all glad they grew up there. They learned to take care of themselves in practical ways. And they learned what is more important: not to judge people by their color, religion, place of origin, or economic status. These things have nothing to do with whether or not you can trust a person.

In the end I learned the wisdom of insecurity in a bitter, heart-breaking way. That same summer of 1964, Sara was Clerk (presiding officer) of the Young Friends of North America, and their delegate to the triennial meeting of the Friends World Committee for Consultation, to be held in Waterford, Ireland, late in June. A week after the accident she would have been on her way to Europe. She also had received a Quaker Leadership Grant to travel for the summer in Europe, with a special concern to visit young Friends in East Germany, Czechoslovakia, and other countries. To facilitate her travels, she had arranged to pick up a Volkswagen bug when she arrived in Europe.

All that spring I had stewed over her plan to go off, at twenty-three, all alone in her little car, behind the Iron Curtain. Who could foresee that only a week before she was to leave she would lose her life on a journey none of us ever questioned?

Chapter I

Emily Dickinson

"Burglar! Banker-Father!"

AS I LAY IN BED that first night in the hospital to which we had been taken, I tried to grasp what had happened. It was all still unreal. Much of the time I was numb, but at others, when the sedatives wore off and I could think clearly, my primary emotion was anger. How could this have happened to us? Though it had been a score of years since I had thought in terms of a personal God who can be invoked for protection and safety, I was outraged at whoever ran the universe so unjustly. I felt betrayed—cut off from contact with God, and I was not sure that the connection could ever be re-established again.[1]

Along with the anger came fear, for it was a fearful and awe-ful thing to be angry at God. Had anyone felt this way before? I remembered Job. He had lost seven sons and three daughters, and he talked back to God. His wife urged him to curse God and die. However in the end he gave in: "Though he slay me, yet will I trust in him." (Job 13:15). I was not sure I could ever trust God again.

Words came to my mind that seemed to express my anger: "Burglar! Banker—Father!" Who had said that? Then I remembered someone who shook her small fist in God's face and told *him* off. Bit by bit the lines came back to me:

I never lost as much but twice,
And that was in the sod.
Twice have I stood a beggar
Before the door of God!

Angels—twice descending
Reimbursed my store—
Burglar! Banker—Father!
I am poor once more! [2]

It was Emily Dickinson who spoke to me that night and made me feel that I was not alone. Back home, some weeks later, I got out her poems and found many more that put words to all that I was feeling. She told God that she felt it futile to pray. She accused God of duplicity. Why are we given people to love, if they are to be arbitrarily taken away from us? Loving human parents do not treat their children so cruelly. The theologians of the 1960's were saying that God was dead. I was inclined to agree with them.

Nor could I find comfort in the idea of the resurrection and eternal life, the theme of most of the sympathy cards which came. Emily agreed with me there, also. She wanted her loved ones with her here and now, not in some dubious future paradise.

The days dragged on, devoid of hope, devoid of color. I went about my accustomed rounds — to work in the morning, back home at night to meal preparation, dishwashing, laundry, and on to bed. What was the point of it all? Emily Dickinson understood that too, how the feet continue to move mechanically through the habits of life and the hours succeed one another leadenly. The fact of death blotted out my awareness of everything else:

> *Circumference without Relief—*
> *Or Estimate—or End—* [3]

It was of some comfort to know that someone else had been in this state before and had recorded it so accurately.

But how could this spinster, this "half-cracked" recluse living out her days with a spinster sister in their father's house, understand all that I was feeling? How could she understand so well what it was to lose a child? I began to read her more carefully. I discovered that though she had not had children of her own, there was a special child in her life.

She had both a brother and a sister — she was the one in the middle. Lavinia, the youngest, shared the house and daily life with her. William Austin, called by his middle name, was the eldest. He had married Susan Gilbert, Emily's girlhood friend, and they lived in the house next door. Father Dickinson had built it for them as a wedding present.

One ponders how the relationship between Emily Dickinson and Susan Gilbert Dickinson must have altered with the years. Close girlhood friends who confide in one another change as they mature and have different experiences. And the relationship definitely changes when that dear friend marries one's brother. A triangle inevitably destroys something of the former intimacy. And later, how hard to realize that this is not a happy marriage, and to speculate where the fault lies.

Austin and Sue had three children: a son, Edward, and then five years later, a daughter, Martha, who grew up to edit some of her aunt's poetry. Then eleven years after that, another son was born. Gilbert was a bright, gifted child, adored by his family and his two aunts next door.

Gilbert died of typhoid fever when he was eight years old. Emily spoke her grief to her sister-in-law in a letter:

> *Dear Sue—*
> *The Vision of Immortal Life has been fulfilled—*

How simply at the last the Fathom comes!
The Passenger and not the Sea, we find sur-
prises us—
Gilbert rejoiced in Secrets—
His Life, was panting with them—with what
menace of Light he cried "Don't tell, Aunt
Emily"! Now my ascended Playmate must in-
struct me. Show us, prattling Preceptor, but the
way to thee!
He knew no niggard moment—His Life was
full of Boon—The Playthings of the Dervish were
not so wild as his—
No crescent was this Creature—He traveled
from the Full—
Such soar, but never set—
I see him in the Star, and meet his sweet
velocity in everything that flies—His Life was
like the Bugle, which winds itself away, his
Elegy an echo—his Requiem ecstasy—
Dawn and Meridian in one.

Wherefore would we wait, wronged only of
Night, which he left for us—
Without a speculation, our little Ajax spans
the whole—

> *Pass to thy Rendezvous of Light,*
> *Pangless except for us—*
> *Who slowly ford the Mystery*
> *Which thou hast leaped across!*

Emily [4]

Years later when I visited the house and garden in Amherst, I felt the presence of a small boy, playing games with his diminutive, child-like aunt, and the two of them bursting with secrets. "Don't tell, Aunt Emily!" With what economy of words she evokes this beloved child: "no niggard moment," "full of boon," "he traveled from the full." Stars remind her of him, and everything that flies brings back "his sweet velocity." His life was "like the bugle." Would I had the gift to evoke my daughter's presence for others, in a few taut phrases, as Emily makes Gilbert live for me.

George and I like to read her poetry aloud. He says, "Her poetry is like a wound-up spring: the compression is the source of the power." Or, to put it another way, she wrote a kind of poetic shorthand. At a superficial reading you may not grasp what she is saying. Each word bears a full load of meaning, but she leaves her readers free to fill the words with added meanings, out of their own experience.

So I ponder the phrases of this letter, and fill them with my own experience. "Such soar, but never set." Sara could soar—that lovely, floating, high soprano voice that could spin out a musical phrase with an unerring sense of the inner meaning of the music, and its timing. But her sun had set at twenty-three before she had time to learn a role and perform in *La Traviata*.

In time Emily's words took on great meaning. There is a garden where a young girl romps with an Irish Setter. Her siblings in the garden with her are in the background, for the memories of them *there* have been superseded by other memories—of their graduations, their marriages, their parenthood. They are growing older. I trust they will live out their full life spans, live to a wise old age. I hope the sun will not go down for them in loss of strength and vigor. But certain it is that the sun will never set on the girl with the dog. Sara will always be twenty-three, young, eager, her face turned toward the future, with "no niggard moment."

And Dickinson is right about learning from children. The preceptors may be "prattling" but unless we keep open to what the young have to teach us, hardening of the mental arteries sets in and we are left on the sidelines. The girl I turned to for companionship, comfort, and advice, still "instructs" me. Of course I turn to the other daughters and to the son for advice and comfort and companionship, and they are all generous with it. But they come and they go. They must be written to and an answer waited for; or they must be phoned, if the need is urgent. And they have their own problems to cope with so I hesitate sometimes to add the additional burden of parental problems. But Sara—still wise, still comforting—has taken up permanent residence. She is available at all hours.

And that other phrase: "Dawn and Meridian in one." I ponder the words and know that I have not yet probed all the layers of meaning in them. How can sunrise and noon be the same? With any child there is the promise and the hope of sunrise that come with birth. To what heights may this young life not soar? Anything is possible! But dawn gives way to the ordinariness of everyday. The glory fades. Ah yes!—Except for those who die young! As the fact of death recedes in time, the beloved child emerges in our lives somewhat larger than life. Our selective memory blots out all the faults, all the imperfections, all the limitations. We remember only "whatsoever things are true, honest, just, pure, lovely, and of good report..." Their promise is fulfilled in blazing noon. For what heights might not this beloved young person snatched from us have reached? Sara might have become a great child psychiatrist—her intended vocation. She might have sung at the Met, if her voice teacher had persuaded her to work full time at her music. She might have written the definitive book or the great poem. She might have done a thousand things. The obstacles, frustrations, pitfalls, limitations, and wrong choices do not exist for those who die young.

And this we owe our beloved dead, whether young or old: to wipe from our memories all that was less than their best, and to carry them in our hearts at their wisest, most compassionate, most creative moments. Is that not what all of us hope from those who survive us—that they will remember us "at the meridian," "soaring, and never setting..."?

And if we owe it to our beloved dead, we also owe it to our beloved living, not to dwell on their faults and lesser moments. In seeing them whole, we help them become more fully themselves.

Time does restore to us our quiet joy in the spiritual presence of those we love, so that we learn to remember without pain, and to speak without choking up with tears. But all our lives we will be subject to sudden small reminders which will bring all the old loss back overwhelmingly, and once again we cry out with Emily Dickinson: "Burglar! Banker—Father! I am poor once more!"

My immersion in Emily Dickinson helped me through the early months of rebellion against God, rage against automobile manufacturers more interested in profits than safe cars, and the American passion for speed. On sleepless nights she was my companion. She became a "guest of my life" at this time, and as I prepared a guest room for her, she settled in and continually threw open the windows and let in fresh air. She became *my* Emily!

But I find she is other peoples' private Emily too. One friend, a midwestern professor whose doctoral dissertation was on Dickinson, and who named her daughter Emily, smiles a Mona Lisa smile when I speak of "my" Emily Dickinson, amused that I should be so bold as to claim possession. Another, a Long Island scholar who writes articles on Dickinson's use of Biblical imagery, raises an eyebrow slightly when I speak of my Emily. Still a third is a New Englander who makes annual pilgrimages to the house in Amherst on Emily's birthday and is part of a select birthday party. She has even handled Emily's teacups! And more people with private Emily Dickinsons keep turning up all the time.

In 1976 I made a trip to New York City to see Julie Harris bring to life her *Belle of Amherst*, a believable Emily Dickinson, without doubt, but still not quite mine.

And somewhere out on the circumference of the universe I hear faint laughter from one who is "all things to all women'' — and to not a few men as well. She has planted her clues so widely and so well that there is an inexhaustible supply of personal Emily Dickinsons to go around for all generations to come.

So I offer here an experiential Emily Dickinson, a sojourner in my life who came to me out of my need, not asking for exhaustive scholarship on my part. (However, I could see being a Dickinson scholar as an enjoyable way of life, if that had been my lot!)

She was born in Amherst, Massachusetts, December 10, 1830, and she lived there all her fifty-six years. Amherst lies in a valley. In one of her more familiar poems she tells us that she never saw the ocean. The mind might range over the universe, but the limits of her physical world were set by the hedge around her house and garden. Housebound, landlocked, she lived her life in ''polar privacy,'' one of the loneliest human beings I know. She once said that she saw ''New Englandly.'' The Connecticut River Valley in which Amherst lies was the center of Puritan settlements. Puritanism looks at human nature, sees both the evil and the good, and then places the emphasis on the evil. Original sin is the central concept. (This is in contrast to Quakerism which places the emphasis on the individual's ''Inner Light,'' or ''that of God.'')

She never joined the church. Enormous pressure was brought on her to confess her sins and to go through the conversion experience, but she never could bring herself to do so. During her lifetime, Emerson and the Transcendentalists challenged the Puritan view of life. She was attracted to their ideas, but her point of view, her frame of reference, was shaped in her girlhood, and she lived her life, as she said, "with a sense of loss."

Having rejected the route to salvation of all her family and friends, she set out to become whole, to become authentic, by herself, by an inward journey. She recognized that those who choose such a path will probably be judged mad by their neighbors, but she didn't care.

The inward journey, celibacy, isolation seemed the only path open because she was a woman. The options for women of her background and family in nineteenth century New England were very few.

When did it begin? Probably in childhood she realized she saw things differently from other people. She saw the irony, the unexpected humor in situations where they could not. She was brighter than her friends; she could write cleverer valentines. This was important, for she was not pretty. Others could get by on their looks; she had to get by on her cleverness.

The only adult photograph we have was taken in 1848 when she was seventeen, a freshman at Mount Holyoke. In it she undoubtedly saw the truth: she was hopelessly plain. She never had another picture taken.

Thomas Wentworth Higginson, with whom she corresponded, asked for a photograph, and she wrote back, "I had no portrait, now, but am small, like the Wren, and my Hair is bold, like the Chestnut Bur, and my eyes, like the Sherry in the Glass, that the Guest leaves." [5] In one of her poems she speaks of herself as being "freckled," and probably meant both literally and figuratively. She was not one of the "saved" who tried to keep themselves "unspotted" by the world.

As a girl she did appear to enjoy going to parties. She loved skating and riding. She seems to have fallen in love several times. And yet, confiding in her girlhood friend, Susan Gilbert, she writes a long letter about brides and "plighted maidens" and girlish dreams of marriage, and then she adds, "It does so rend me, Susie, the thought of it when it comes, that I tremble lest at sometime I, too, am yielded up." [6]

Could she ever have given up her own self-contained privacy, her individuality, to anyone? The poems suggest a passionate romance with someone unavailable, probably married to someone else. Much research has been done to identify this person, or persons, and there are a number of likely candidates, people to whom she was drawn. I think it likely that if she fell in love it would have had to be with someone unavailable. Because marriage would be out of the range of possibility, the problem of yielding herself up was solved. Sometimes I wonder whether there was a real lover, whether the passionate romance of the poems is a vicarious one, a product of her vivid imagination, with just enough clues thrown in to make it plausible. Could it all have been a smokescreen to throw future scholars off the trail? What an interesting game to play. How she would have enjoyed it. And who knows, really? She was confident that fame would eventually find her.

I do not think she ever could have yielded herself up to any man. For all her daughterly devotion to her father, her descriptions of him in her letters to brother Austin away at Harvard Law School prick his pomposity behind his back. The household might revolve around Father, and Emily be the dutiful daughter ever alert to bring the slippers, but she is amused by him. He may command her obedience, but he cannot control her mind.

One by one her friends married. It was hard to keep going to social gatherings in a close-knit community where people gossip about your plainness and continued singleness. How much easier to stay home and not try to keep up appearances.

So she chose solitude. The Dickinson house is large and the hedge surrounds spacious grounds. The house is topped by a cupola with windows on four sides. Here she could observe Amherst in detached curiosity, without personal involvement. It proved a good place to write.

Writing verses had always come easily. Now, in young womanhood, with marriage out of the picture, she worked at her craft and became aware of her creative gift. As confidence grew, she realized that for her to be a poet was a far greater fate than to be a wife and mother. And as the poetry poured from her brain and her pen, she knew, beyond doubt, that her gift was authentic.

Solitude was self-chosen also because the creative gift demanded it. The normal contacts and interruptions that fill up a woman's day interrupt the flow of inspiration. A gift can be frittered away, one's time to write evaporate, unless privacy is guarded jealously. I know this experientially. And in addition, she was never robust. The contacts with other people drained her energy. How much easier to write them little notes, or send a few flowers from her garden with a poem.

She lived in a world run by men, for men. Women had few rights and scant recognition. She knew she was more intelligent, more perceptive, more creative than most, if not all, the men she knew. She knew that her gift was unique, and she would not yield it to anyone's domination. And yet, it would be nice to have confirmation of the gift by someone competent to judge.

In April 1862 she saw an article in the *Atlantic Monthly* called, "To a Young Contributor," by Thomas Wentworth Higginson, former army colonel, minister, and now writer and lecturer. It was a letter of advice to young would-be poets, and on the whole the advice was not bad if you wanted to write publishable verse in the 19th century. Emily decided to write to him. She picked out some of her poems that she thought fitted his guidelines. In fact she probably wrote some specifically to fit them. Higginson said, "Charge your style with life," and in the covering letter she asked him if her verses "breathed."

Higginson also said in the article that it would be a great privilege to discover a new poetic genius.

Poor man! He failed to recognize one when she materialized before him, and he is chiefly remembered today because of his obtuseness. He told her her poems could not be published with their imperfect rhymes, and erratic metric beat.

She continued to write to him for years, sending him more poems to criticize. She had a wonderful time leading him on, signing herself tongue-in-cheek, "your scholar," but of course she never took his advice.

Why did she pick someone second rate to write to for advice? The New England woods were full of genuine poets: Bryant, Lowell, Holmes, Whittier, Longfellow. Emerson, probably the most original of them, had even been a guest in Austin's house next door. Why did she not approach him? Walt Whitman had sent him a copy of *Leaves of Grass* when the first edition was off the press, and had received by return mail the confirmation of his gift, "I greet you at the beginning of a great career."

Emily called Higginson her "safest friend." Was she afraid of success and recognition because of the harrowing early pressure on her to confess her sins, because the Puritan climate of her youth caused her to live with a sense of loss, without expectation of bliss? This may have been part of it, but there is more.

To approach Emerson whose gifts and perception were exceptional would be dangerous for her. His criticism and advice probably would have been encouraging and astute, and by objective standards, helpful. It would have meant, however, yielding a portion of her vision and her gift into his keeping. It was safer not to risk it.

After Higginson's negative verdict, she gave up hope of publishing in her lifetime. The few times she had submitted poems for publication, some uninspired editor made them rhyme properly and perhaps otherwise tampered with their authenticity. The only fame that she could accept was her own inner certainty that the poems were right. She did not need criticism. She had her own inner monitor. She said that if the top of her head seemed to come off, she knew her words were right.

She felt secure about the ultimate recognition and the permanence of her life's work. She began copying the poems she considered finished on clean paper and she bound groups of related verses into little hand-sewn booklets, or ''fascicles.'' Recognition could wait for eternity.

Lavinia found the treasure after her death. There were 1775 poems, about half of them sewn into fascicles, and several hundred more in loose packets.

The rest were scribbled on old envelopes or other scraps of paper, some in pencil and almost illegible, and some unfinished with alternate words in the margins.

Lavinia entrusted this precious legacy to a neighbor, Mabel Loomis Todd, who worked with Col. Higginson (who else?) to copy them into readable form, and, yes, to edit them and make them publishable. (Emily's punctuation, consisting mainly of dashes, and grammar were individual and eccentric, like her rhyme and meter.) Together Mrs. Todd and Col. Higginson brought out several volumes of the poems, and they met with a wide audience. They saw they had a market, so they published some of her correspondence, with tantalizing omissions. And the myths about Emily Dickinson began to grow.

Then the Todd and Dickinson families became embroiled in a law suit. Austin Dickinson left Mrs. Todd a piece of property in his will. Perhaps he wanted to compensate her for all the work she had done on the poetry. Lavinia had been tight-fisted about the royalties. Or perhaps he had been romantically interested in Mrs. Todd, since his marriage was not happy. In any case, Lavinia brought suit to keep Mabel Todd from getting the legacy, and won the case.

In anger and disgust Mrs. Todd locked in a trunk in the attic all the poems not yet released for publication, and there they sat for decades. They survived a hurricane and a fire before they finally came to rest in the Harvard archives. It was 1944 before the last of them were published.

Emily Dickinson could not and would not yield her poetic gift into any man's keeping, as she could not have yielded herself personally in marriage, I believe, despite the anguished poetry. And I find that she also had difficulty yielding herself to a male God. After many of the girls at Mount Holyoke had been converted, Mary Lyon, head of the school, asked all those who at least *desired* to become Christians to stand. Emily was the only one to remain seated. She felt that it might look strange to be the lone holdout, but that dishonesty would be worse. As I read the poems, I realize that at times this estrangement from salvation was frightening, but I am left with the impression that more often it was amusing.

And the same inner authenticity that served as her guide as to what was right in her poetry characterized her relationship to deity. The only way she could establish the connection to God was on the basis of complete honesty. When she felt misused, as when she felt amused, she claimed the right to say so. What enormous courage and sense of one's personhood it must have taken to approach God with such utter honesty. I did not know it at the time, but she was paving the way for my own reestablishing of a relationship to God.

The neighbors may have thought of her as "Squire Dickinson's half-cracked daughter," but she loved her life and found it fulfilling.

> *I dwell in Possibility—*
> *A fairer House than Prose—*
> *More numerous of Windows—*
> *Superior—for Doors—*
>
> *Of Chambers as the Cedars—*
> *Impregnable of Eye—*
> *And for an Everlasting Roof*
> *The Gambrels of the Sky—*
>
> *Of Visitors—the fairest—*
> *For Occupation—This—*
> *The spreading wide my narrow Hands*
> *To gather Paradise—* [7]

Emily Dickinson gave special meanings to some words. One of these was *circumference*. Circumference is the ultimate boundary of wholeness, whether the circle it contains is tiny or tremendous.

> *When Bells stop ringing—Church—begins—*
> *The Positive—of Bells—*

When Cogs—stop—that's Circumference—
The Ultimate—of Wheels. [8]

When we pause in the daily round of cogs mesh-
ing into one another, the trivial busyness that makes
up so much of our lives, we can become aware of the
great wheel of the Universe turning with its circumference in the far reaches of space.

When she had experienced the utmost depths of
loneliness, a privacy that would not yield itself up to
anyone, even to God, she was given to see the wholeness of the universe contained within its circumference:

I saw no Way—The Heavens were stitched—
I felt the Columns close—
The Earth reversed her Hemispheres—
I touched the Universe—

And back it slid—and I alone—
A Speck upon a Ball—
Went out upon Circumference—
Beyond the Dip of Bell— [9]

And on the circumference of my world she remains. She taught me that grief is a time to be lived
through, experienced fully, and that the heavens will
not fall if I give voice to my anger against God in
such a time. When we accept the unacceptable, it

has no more power over us. We can move through and beyond the experience.

She taught me to trust myself as a woman, and to get on with creating my own wholeness. She was an excellent companion as I became aware of the emerging women's liberation movement and she prepared my entry into it.

She suggested that I seek a larger God than the Judeo-Christian "God the Father" we both inherited. I have begun to glimpse a God larger than human sexuality, in whom light and darkness, inwardness and outwardness, maleness and femaleness are interdependent parts. Is that, perhaps, what she meant by "that Assembly—not far off/From furthest Spirit—God"? Or did she mean our beloved dead who are in time in some measure restored to us as continuing presences in our lives?

She came to me at a time when "the heavens were stitched" for me. She is a "guest-in-residence" with a permanent guestroom assigned to her. And she continues to enlighten and dazzle and stretch me to reach toward my own circumference.

On a Columnar Self—
How ample to rely
In Tumult—or Extremity—
How good the Certainty

That Lever cannot pry—
And Wedge cannot divide
Conviction—That Granitic Base
Though None be on our Side—

Suffice Us—for a Crowd—
Ourself—and Rectitude—
And that Assembly—not far off
From furthest Spirit—God— [10]

Chapter II

Rainer Maria Rilke

"Over the nowhere
arches the everywhere."

EMILY DICKINSON, my companion in the early months of grief, wrote:

We grow accustomed to the Dark—
When Light is put away— ...
Either the Darkness alters—
Or something in the sight
Adjusts itself to Midnight—
And Life steps almost straight. [1]

And so it was. We began to recover in body and in mind; life resumed something of its normal pace. I went through the routines of home and job. I functioned. But the world was still drained of color. An enormous shadow fell between me and the sun. Grief, being never absent, still determined the circumference of my world. And God was still dead.

Then in the spring, some nine months after the accident, a friend sent me a poem by Rainer Maria Rilke. I had heard the name, knew that he wrote in German, but that was about all. Now this poem began to haunt me:

Everything beckons to us to perceive it,
murmurs at every turn, "Remember me!"

A day we passed, too busy to receive it,
will yet unlock us all its treasury.

Who shall compute our harvest? Who shall bar
us from the former years, the long-departed?
What have we learnt from living since we started,
except to find in others what we are?

Except to re-enkindle commonplace?
O house, O sloping field, O setting sun!
Your features form into a face, you run,
you cling to us, returning our embrace!

One space spreads through all creatures equally—
inner-world-space. Birds quietly flying go
flying through us. O, I that want to grow!
the tree I look outside at's growing in me!

I have a house within when I need care.
I have a guard within when I need rest.
The love that I have had!—Upon my breast
the beauty of the world clings, to weep there. [2]

Phrases from the poem came to me as I worked, as I walked, as I woke at night.

Who shall compute our harvest? Who shall bar
us from the former years...

The answer, Rilke seemed to imply, was no one, no one except myself. I asked myself, was it possible that the treasure of days passed by could still be recovered?

I have a house within…

Had I been looking in the wrong direction? Everything *outside* reminded me of my loss, for memories are associated with places and things. If I could learn to look within, could I find her still there?

…a house within when I need care.
…a guard within when I need rest.
The love that I have had!

Did that love still exist as a two-way relationship so that it could shelter me like a house, and let me relax without having to be on guard?

One space spreads through all creatures equally—
inner—world—space…

In preoccupation with my own grief, I was failing to see the inner-world-space of those around me. I remembered mystical experiences I had had, and I longed to be open to them again, vulnerable enough to experience once more the wholeness of life.

—Upon my breast
the beauty of the world clings, to weep there.

All things carry the seeds of death in them, of separation, of longing. In their fragility lies their beauty. My private grief had kept blinding me to the fact that everyone, and everything, is finite.

Rilke's poem seemed to imply a larger world than the one in which I lived. It appeared to be a world in which the past continues into the present so that it becomes a part of it (and the future, too, as I was to experience.) The inner world and the outer are parts of a whole—with no separation. And the living and the dead (and the as yet unborn) are a beloved community. All this seemed to be implied in the poem as I lived with it day after day.

I am given to enthusiasms. As I had immersed myself in Dickinson, so I now immersed myself in Rilke. It was not that my love for Emily faded, but that Rainer seemed to provide the other side of the coin. Dickinson was concerned with personal authenticity. Rilke seemed to be concerned with the authenticity of everyone and everything else.

How could I climb out of my two-dimensional world into his multi-dimensional one? The opening line of the poem suggested the way:

Everything beckons to us to perceive it...

Grief had kept me from perceiving. It got in the way of seeing things, hearing things, responding to things. It was spring again now. All around me, I realized, things were murmuring, "Remember me!"

A line from another poem became my touchstone:

There remains, perhaps,
some tree on a slope, to be looked at day after day. [3]

Slopes are not easily come by in Chicago, but I found my tree, a Japanese maple, and I began to perceive it day after day, season after season. As my acquaintance with the tree, and with Rilke, grew, so did my perception. The shadow of grief began to lift. A line from another poem began to describe my emergence into the light of affirmation again:

Over the nowhere arches the everywhere. [4]

But who was Rilke? Even before I felt sufficiently acquainted with him to make claims to a personal Rilke, as I had my private Emily, I found that other people had their private Rilkes. C.F. MacIntyre begins his Introduction to his translation of *Selected Poems:*

"After I had got on with my personal Rilke for ten years, I was surprised to discover I'd been living with a sort of Proteus who seems to have been all things to all critics and to have trifled with me,...After some melancholy months of perturbation, during which time I have regarded his disaffections as personal disloyalty, I have been able to put most of these Rilkes aside in my mind...

"I want now to isolate my own Rilke, with a documented brief for his existence, as a man who during a certain period of his life rode the twin fillies of the wing'd horse, sculpture and painting, keeping a firm foot on each, and singing, as he went, his beautifully formed and colored sonnets, or polishing and painting small concert and salon pieces, sonatas in miniature." [5]

I cannot document my Rilke as thoroughly as MacIntyre can his, but I want to affirm that he does exist, that he is alive and well and occupying a permanent guest room in my house. And I find that a casual reference to him, or even a line quoted out of context, will often reward me with an answering gleam in another's eye. People of many ages, and many occupations, and many dispositions, have their private Rilkes about whom they feel strongly.

Out of what kind of human life had this unusual poetry and this compelling vision of the universe come? I could not get very deeply into the poetry without wanting to know more about the poet.

Emily Dickinson withdrew into her house and

garden to shut out distractions and to experience life more intensely. Rilke did not have a permanent home until the last years of his life. He was a wanderer, and he wrote much of his poetry as a guest in other homes.

Like Dickinson, he gave his own meaning to special words. The most important of them was not a grand word like "circumference," but a humble one. It is *thing*. Its meaning has its roots in his childhood. He speaks in his second lecture on Rodin of those things to which small children, even babies, attach themselves—teddy bears, dolls, blankets—without which they are inconsolable, cannot settle down to sleep, and to which they cling even after they become ragged and worn out and broken. This childhood thing dominates life and is in many ways more important than people. He adds:

> *This small forgotten object, that was ready to signify everything, made you intimate with thousands through playing a thousand parts, being animal and tree and king and child—and when it withdrew, they were all there. This Something, worthless as it was, prepared your relationships with the world, it guided you into happening and among people, and, further: you experienced through it, through its existence, through its anyhow-appearance, through its final smashing or*

*its enigmatic departure, all that is human, right
into the depths of death.*[6]

Rilke was born December 4, 1875, in Prague, then still part of the Austro-Hungarian Empire. He was the product of an unhappy marriage. His father had wanted a military career, but had had to settle for a dull civil service job. His mother felt she had married beneath herself when the dashing young officer in uniform turned into an ordinary and undistinguished white-collar worker. Rilke saw her as arrogant, and difficult, and very pious. There is some evidence that she was not as negative a person as this poem would indicate, but certainly much of the time this is how he perceived her:

*Alas, my mother will demolish me!
Stone after stone upon myself I'd lay,
and stood already like a little house round which
    the day
rolls boundlessly.
Now mother's coming to demolish me:*

*demolish me by simply being there.
That building's going on she's unaware.
Through my stone wall she passes heedlessly.
alas, my mother will demolish me!*

*In lighter flight the birds encircle me.
The strange dogs know already: this is he.*

It's hidden only from my mother's glance,
my gradually augmented countenance.

No warm wind ever blew to me from her.
She's not at home where breezes are astir.
In some heart-attic she is tucked away,
And Christ comes there to wash her every day. [7]

Poor boy! No wonder he placed such importance on a childhood "thing." He really needed a security blanket! The tragedy is that this poem was written when he was forty. Alas, his mother outlived him. Though she did not recognize his "augmented countenance" when he needed that recognition, she did live to bask in the reflected glory of his fame.

Sophia Rilke had lost an infant daughter before Rainer was born. She dressed her man child in girls' clothes until he went to school. At ten he was sent away from home to a military school. His fellow students made fun of him and he retreated into himself. Finally his frail health allowed him to escape the nightmare. He was sent to business school, but he had as little aptitude for that as for the army. He tried the university at Prague, but soon dropped out of that too. In 1899, he and Lou Andreas-Salome journeyed together to Russia. They met and were deeply impressed by Tolstoy. They studied Russian over the winter and made a longer Russian tour the next spring. In Rilke's mind the Russian experience marked the beginning of his spiritual and artistic development. A score of years later in one of the *Sonnets to Orpheus*, he evokes the memory of an evening in Russia, and a white horse joyfully tossing his mane, despite the hobble on his leg, as he was turned out to pasture on a Volga meadow. He sent the sonnet to Lou.

In 1900 he moved for a time to a colony of artists at Worpswede in Germany. Here he met and married Clara Westhoff, the sculptor. They went to Paris in 1902, drawn by their mutual interest in Auguste Rodin. Rilke served as Rodin's secretary for a time, and wrote a book on him. Rodin, like Tolstoy, was a major influence in his artistic development. Sculpture finds its way into his poetry all through the many volumes.

The poetry of these early Paris years established Rilke as a major voice. He evolved a new kind of poetry, which he called his "thing poems." (*Ding Gedichte*) Rodin's method of working impressed him. Rodin approached a piece of marble, not with preconceived ideas, but open to the possibilities that lay within the block of stone, possibilities that his hands could reveal. Both Rodin and Rilke wondered if this were applicable to poetry as well as to sculpture. They drew up a list of "things" in and around Paris which might presumably yield poems. Rilke systematically exposed himself to one thing after another on the list, waiting perceptively for each to yield its poem to him. The first poem he thought successful was about the panther in the zoo in Le Jardin des Plantes:

> *His sight from ever gazing through the bars*
> *has grown so blunt that it sees nothing more.*
> *It seems to him that thousands of bars are*
> *before him, and behind them nothing merely.*
>
> *The easy motion of his supple stride,*
> *which turns about the very smallest circle,*
> *is like a dance of strength about a center*
> *in which a mighty will stands stupefied.*
>
> *Only sometimes when the pupil's film*
> *soundlessly opens...then one image fills*
> *and glides through the quiet tension of the limbs*
> *into the heart and ceases and is still.* [8]

Swans, flamingoes, gazelles, the merry-go-round in the park, blue hydrangeas — the thing poems poured forth. Notre Dame, DaVinci's fresco of the Last Supper, Roman sarcophagi, early Greek sculpture in the Louvre, paintings — especially those of Cezanne — all yielded their poetry to him. Rodin's sculpture, of course, was another fertile source. Several poems derive from Rodin's "Hand of God," as this one:

> *The leaves fall, fall as if from far away,*
> *like withered things from gardens deep in sky;*
> *they fall with gestures of renunciation.*
>
> *And through the night the heavy earth falls too,*
> *down from the stars, into the loneliness.*
>
> *And we all fall. This hand must fall.*
> *Look everywhere: it is the lot of all.*
>
> *Yet there is one who holds us as we fall*
> *eternally in his hands' tenderness.* [9]

It was a fruitful time. *The Book of Pictures* was published in July 1902, and a second edition with additional poems in December 1906. *The Book of Hours*, whose imaginary author is a Russian monk, appeared in 1905. *New Poems* came out in December 1907, and *New Poems, Second Part*, in November 1908. These Paris years also saw his one major prose work published, *The Notebooks of Malte Laurids Brigge*. There are vivid pictures of things in it, too. The passage on Beethoven's death mask is especially moving to me, for I felt something of the same emotions when I saw it in Vienna in 1970, but had no words to express them.

In spite of the productivity, it was a difficult and insecure time for Rilke. The position as Rodin's secretary was not really satisfactory to either of them. Like Dickinson, he was called to be a poet, and like her, he had to give up everything else if he were to fulfill his calling. There seemed no way to earn a living and support his wife and child and still have the necessary time and concentration to write. He and Clara gave up a household together. Their small daughter, Ruth, was raised by Clara's parents. Clara pursued her career as a sculptor. They were never divorced; they wrote to one another, though with less frequency and intimacy as the years advanced.

Rilke found it difficult to establish permanent relations with anyone. Some of the most brilliant and beautiful women of Europe were his intimate friends, and sometimes lovers. They lent him their villas for periods of solitude to write. Paris was home for him, but he also travelled widely, with memorable journeys to Italy, Spain, and Egypt. Imagery from these journeys became the substance of poetry. C.F. MacIntyre, in the same introduction in which he isolated his private Rilke, says of these Paris years:

"The most important poet in Germany since Goethe, let him be considered at this period of his life as a man who felt himself in exile, a man who spent his days in museums, galleries, studios, libraries, public parks and gardens; a wanderer of the streets by night, often even of the more sinister boulevards, a brooder on the many bridges over the Seine."[10]

The periods of creativity would suddenly end, however, and times of dryness set in, and then he despaired that his poetic gift was irrevocably gone. In these times he was a prolific correspondent, and the letters are beautiful reading. His friend, the Austrian essayist, Rudolf Kassner, suggested that Rilke's poetry and his correspondence are like a coat and its lining. The lining is made of such beautiful material that one is tempted to wear the garment inside out.

A student in the same military school in Prague that Rilke had endured as a boy, wrote him to ask for criticism of his own poetry. Franz Xaver Kappus never did become a well known poet, but he is remembered because he preserved and published ten letters Rilke wrote him between 1903 and 1908, under the title, *Letters to a Young Poet*. They are full of grace and wisdom and are a good place to start for those who do not know Rilke and would like to become acquainted with his style and ideas.

He began to feel a great work stirring within him. A friend invited him to spend the winter of 1911-12 at her castle, overlooking the Adriatic. The hospitable family would not be at Castle Duino and he could have the solitude he needed. But the weeks wore on and the muse was absent. An annoying business letter came one day, demanding an answer, and it seemed to be the final detail in his despair. He went out into the wind and walked along the edge of the cliff over the sea, and his despair found voice:

Who, if I cried, would hear me among the angelic orders? [11]

These are the opening words of the ''First Duino Elegy.'' Part of the answer that came to him there on the cliff was:

There remains, perhaps, some tree on a slope, to be looked at day after day...

He completed the first elegy that evening. Within the next month he finished the second, and fragments of others. And then inspiration ran out. This was 1912, and the terrible events of the world were to create for him, as for so many others, an enormous hiatus.

Paris was still home base, but at the precise moment the hostilities of the First World War broke out, he was on holiday in Germany. As an Austrian national, he could not return to France. He camped out most of the war years in Munich. His Paris landlady auctioned off the possessions in his apartment — his letters and pictures, even, and all the precious little "things." He was called up for military service, and even had a few terrible days of drill which brought back the old boyhood nightmare. Friends intervened and arranged a desk job, but it would appear that he was not very efficient at it. It was a time to be endured.

In the summer of 1914, he wrote two related poems — related, at least, in my mind. The first he wrote in Paris on June 20th, before the war began, and the second in Munich during late August and early September. He sent the first poem to his friend Lou Andreas-Salome, the companion of his youthful Russian journeys, saying, "…I spontaneously called it 'Turning,' because it depicts *the* turning which probably must come if I am to live…" [12]

In the poem he looks back on the years of writing the "thing poems" as a time of "gazing" in detachment. He speaks of himself in the third person as the gazer, and speaks of stars, towers, landscapes, captive lions, birds, flowers he has gazed into while he waited for their poetry to emerge. Then he speaks of his wandering, his restlessness, his inability to write, and the depressing inns where he cannot sleep. He feels judgment has been passed on him that he has gazed into things but has not loved them, and this is why he can no longer write. Then he addresses himself directly:

> *Work of sight is done,*
> *now do heart-work*
> *on the pictures within you, those captives; for you*
> *overcame them: but now do not know them.*
> *Behold, inner man, your inner maiden,*
> *this, won from*
> *a thousand natures, this*
> *creature, now only won,*
> *never yet loved.* [13]

The poem he wrote two months later is the one my friend sent me that spring after the accident. In both poems the birds are flying through him. He gave no title to this poem. At the beginning of this chapter I quoted the poem in the translation in which my friend sent it to me. The last stanza, which moved me deeply, read:

I have a house within when I need care.
I have a guard within when I need rest.
The love that I have had!—Upon my breast
the beauty of the world clings, to weep there.

In later editions, however, the translator, J.B. Leishman, had second thoughts. He retranslated those last four lines so that they now read:

It stands in me, that house I look for still,
in me that shelter I have not possessed.
I, the now well-beloved: on my breast
this fair world's image clings and weeps her fill.[14]

This seemed to change the meaning for me. I had read into the earlier translation that the only real shelter or dwelling we have is the love we have given and received. The second translation does not seem to say that, at least not as clearly as the first. So I worked to make a literal translation:

I shelter myself; in me is the house.
I guard myself and in me is the guard.
Beloved that I have become, on me rests
the lovely image of creation, crying itself out.

This seemed to confirm the second translation and I was disappointed. But as I became more deeply involved in Rilke's life, this second translation took on new meaning. During the war, Castle Duino, where the first of the elegies had been written, was bombed and destroyed. Rilke managed to complete the fourth elegy, the most pessimistic one, during the war. But he came to feel that he must find the right place to bring the project to completion, some place untouched by the war. In such a place, with a sufficient time of solitude and concentration, he believed the elegies would come right. During the war he despaired that he would ever find such a place and time. There is a special poignancy, then, in Leishman's second translation:

It stands in me, that house I look for still...

In 1919 an invitation came to lecture in Switzerland. It seemed a good omen. Perhaps here he would find the right place. Eventually he found a diminutive 13th century castle — run down, with no water or electricity, but with a magnificent view of the Rhone valley. Castle Muzot felt right, although the practical problems of making it liveable loomed large for a while. All through the summer of 1921 friends helped make it habitable, and as fall gave way to winter, and he adjusted his habits to his new home, he felt certain he could achieve here the necessary concentration to complete the long interrupted work.

And he was right. In February 1922, in a burst of

inspiration that held him day and night, he completed the ten elegies, and was satisfied that they were right. In addition a sequence of fifty-five sonnets came to him, fully formed, and needing little revision. The genesis of the sonnets had come on New Year's Day when he read a friend's account of the death of her daughter from a mysterious glandular disorder. Vera Knoop was a dancer. Rilke remembered her. She was only nineteen when she died. The *Sonnets to Orpheus* are in her memory.

There remained a few more years, lived for the most part in his small castle. He wrote, but no longer under pressure nor with such intensity. His health was failing. In time his malady was diagnosed as leukemia. He died on December 29, 1926, and is buried in the yard of an old church near Muzot, where the view of the valley was unusually lovely. It was a place dear to him, and he chose it.

In a poem of the Paris years, called "Remembering," he spoke of a year's "anguish, and form, and prayer." The word translated *form* is *gestalt*. Anguish, form, prayer—this is a brief summary of his life. The breadth of his vision is measured by the depth of his loneliness, his periods of despair and anguish. The shape his poetry took was determined by his lifelong preoccupation with form and pattern in other art media. And always he remains, as I see him, the great God-seeker.

In the Paris years, again, he wrote one of the greatest "thing poems" about an ancient torso of Apollo in the Louvre. The beauty of this broken fragment is so perfect, so complete in itself, that having once seen it, he says, you can never be the same again: *You must change your life*. I, too, was confronted in Rilke's poetry with beauty that left me no place to hide. I had to change my life.

I moved out of the "nowhere" of grief, into the "everywhere" of affirmation of life. I began to see that everything was asking to be responded to, to be remembered. Relationships are a trust, a responsibility to which we are called, as he said. Our first obligation is to respond to the content of each given moment perceptively. So I strive, imperfectly, to live.

I had not gone far before I discovered that Rilke had much to say about those who die young—"the early departed" as it is sometimes translated, or "the youthfully dead." The first elegy has many beautiful lines which suggest what it must be like for those who die before their time, no longer having human relationships. Then he adds:

> *Yes, but all of the living*
> *make the mistake of drawing too sharp distinctions.*

Angels (they say) are often unable to tell
whether they move among living or dead. The eternal
torrent whirls all the ages through either realm
for ever, and sounds above their voices in both. [15]

In time my daughter came back to me as a living presence in my life—not in any supernatural way, but experienced as warmth, like sunlight.

Rilke wrote a long poem, "Requiem for a Friend," in memory of Paula Modersohn-Becker. Paula Becker and Clara Westhoff were close friends in the artists' community at Worpswede. Paula was perhaps the most gifted artist there. Soon after Clara and Rainer were married, Paula married Otto Modersohn, another member of the colony. He was a pleasant, but mediocre artist. The marriage was not happy. Modersohn found it hard to accept his wife's greater gift. Paula felt stifled by marriage and knew that her creativity was being destroyed by the relationship. She left her husband and went to Paris in 1906. Later that year, he followed her and persuaded her to return to him. She died in 1907 in childbirth.

Rilke was haunted by the tragedy. Paula Becker's problem was his own: the claim of one's artistic calling, and the conflicting claims of one's personal relationships. He felt strongly the wrongness of

Modersohn's insistence that his wife return to him, and in the Requiem he says:

For this is guilt, if anything be guilt,
not to enlarge the freedom of a love
with all the freedom in one's own possession.
All we can offer where we love is this:
to loose each other;... [16]

Hard words for parents and lovers!

The poem for Paula Becker led me to the astounding discovery of Rilke the feminist. As I became part of the women's movement in the late 1960's and early 1970's, I found that I was companioned not only by Emily Dickinson, but by Rainer Maria Rilke as well. He speaks in many places of right relationships between men and women. The most familiar one is in the seventh "Letter to a Young Poet" where the protection of one another's solitude is given as the right commitment in a love relationship.

Rilke gave me a greater gift, however. Through living with his arresting poetry I entered once again into a creative relationship with God—a God more beautiful, more mysterious, more personal than I had known.

Rilke's God is a very personal one—the God of an artist with a perceiving eye and a mystical sensitivity. He tells of a conversation about God that he and

Paula Becker had. She identified God with nature, which she thought of in feminine terms as the source of life. Rilke still saw God in masculine pronouns. God is still growing, he said, and needs our help. Due to his state of incompleteness, God has inconsistencies, even shortcomings.

Reality for Rilke lies in relationships. Everything needs the perceiving response to attain wholeness:

Until I perceived it, no thing was complete,
but waited, hushed, unfulfilled. [17]

And this is no less true of God, he says, than of created things:

What will you do, God, when I die?
When I, your pitcher, broken, lie?
When I, your drink, go stale and dry?
I am your garb, the trade you ply,
you lose your meaning, losing me. [18]

This whole idea is not too inconsistent with that of the theologian under whom I did my graduate work at the University of Chicago Divinity School. Henry Nelson Wieman saw God as "creative interchange," that extra component in a relationship which makes it more than the sum total of its parts. Wieman said we need to be sensitively, intelligently, and appreciatively present in all our relationships, in so far as we can.

Rilke had vivid mystical experiences from time to time. One of these took place at Duino that winter he began the Elegies. He told his friend who owned the castle about it later. He was standing on the roots of an old olive tree, leaning against its trunk. The sensation came to him that everything that had ever lived or suffered existed in him. He felt the anguish and the love of all human existence, and non-human existence as well, concentrated in him.

I was fortunate that the first book I owned by Rilke was *The Book of Hours*, translated by Babette Deutsch, herself a poet. This was the one available at the bookstore when I went in to ask for something by Rilke. Deutsch has been quite faithful to the original text, but her translations come out poetry in their own right. *The Book of Hours* was exactly what I needed at that time. Thanks to Emily Dickinson my anger against God was now largely spent. I was longing to establish a relationship again and I was groping for a way.

The only way we can communicate our experience of God is through symbols. They come thick and fast in *The Book of Hours*. The book encouraged me to search for my own symbols, to create them out of my experience, transforming the outward stimulation into inner meaning. It became for me a form of praying, a practice of the presence of God. And God, who had been dead for me, became resurrected in me.

> *You have so mild a way of being.*
> *They*
> *who name you loudly when they come to pray*
> *forget your nearness.* [19]

Poetry can be a means to religious experience.

In 1970, I had a long bout with pneumonia. During the long nights when I struggled to breathe, these lines sustained me:

> *You, neighbor God, if sometimes in the night*
> *I rouse you with loud knocking, I do so*
> *only because I seldom hear you breathe*
> *and know: you are alone.*
> *And should you need a drink, no one is there*
> *to reach it to you, groping in the dark.*
> *Always I hearken. Give but a small sign.*
> *I am quite near.* [20]

This strange inversion of our usual conception intrigued me: as if God were the pneumonia patient, struggling to breathe, groping in the dark for a drink. In time I came to realize that Neighbor God was not only suffering from pneumonia in my room, but from many things in many rooms.

The most arresting symbol for God that I have found in Rilke is a bouncing ball. Rilke was intrigued by balls, and the figure recurs in poem after poem. I found it first in *The Book of Hours*:

If I had grown up in a land where days
were free from care and hours were delicate,
then I would have contrived a splendid fête
for you, and not have held you in the way
I sometimes do, tightly in fearful hands.

There I would have been bold to squander you,
you boundless Presence.
Like a ball
I would have flung you among all tossing joys,
so one might catch you,
and if you seemed to fall,
with both hands high would spring
toward you,
you thing of things.[21]

The ball appears again in one of the poems of his last summer, a poem sent on August 24, 1926 to Erika Mitterer, a friend with whom he corresponded in verse:

Dove that remained outside,   outside the dovecote,
back in its sphere and home,   one with the day and
*   night,*
it knows the secrecy   when the most remote
terror is fused into   deeply felt flight.

Of all the doves the   always most protected,
never endangered most,   does not know tenderness;
richest of all hearts is   the resurrected;
turning back liberates,   freedom rejoices.

Over the nowhere   arches the everywhere.
Oh, the ball that is   thrown, that we dare,
does it not fill our hands   differently than before?
By the weight of return   it is more. [22]

So I think of the daughter to whom at birth I promised the freedom to leave the dovecote. And I think of myself, resurrected from grief, and I rejoice that I left the nowhere for the everywhere that contains us both. And I pray for courage not to cling too tightly to any ball that is tossed into my eager hands.

I began my journey with Rilke by finding a tree:

> *There remains, perhaps,*
> *some tree on a slope, to be looked at day after*
> *   day...*

and I found, as he found in Munich in the terrible days of the war, that

> *the tree I look outside at grows in me!*

And the tree became a symbol of my world. So each of us may look without and within, perceptively, discerning our own patterns and overlapping relationships, and out of them constructing our own symbols of reality, while we still have time to perceive them.

> Whoever you are, go out into the evening,
> leaving your room, of which you know each bit;
> your house is the last before the infinite,
> whoever you are.
> Then with your eyes that wearily
> scarce lift themselves from the worn-out doorstone
> slowly you raise a shadowy black tree
> and fix it on the sky: slender, alone.
> And you have made the world (and it shall grow
> and ripen as a word, unspoken, still).
> When you have grasped its meaning with your will,
> then tenderly your eyes will let it go...[23]

Chapter III

Katherine Mansfield

"All is well."

SPEAKING OF THOSE who died young, Rilke asks:

What they require of me? I must gently remove
    the appearance
of suffered injustice, that hinders
a little, at times, their purely-proceeding spirits.[1]

Rainer Maria Rilke had helped to restore to me the spiritual presence of my daughter, and so the cloud of grief had lifted. But he was right in his question about "the youthfully dead." I still felt keenly the injustice of having life cut off abruptly at twenty-three. I had recovered from grief and had re-entered life. But there is no re-entry for those who die young. I kept feeling the injustice from Sara's imagined point of view.

I kept asking myself how a young person feels who knows she is going to die. Then I remembered having read Katherine Mansfield's *Journal* in college. She had courageously faced death at an early age. I got out the book and lived with it for weeks. I drew books about Katherine Mansfield from the library and reread the short stories.

Of all these "guests of my life," I identify most with Katherine. She is my kind of person. I think I understand her from the inside. Dickinson's solitariness and Rilke's restless wandering and despair were not her problems, as they are not mine. Katherine's frustrations and fears are like my own, only greatly intensified. And I have been seriously ill with a lung disease and can imagine sympathetically the much greater suffering tuberculosis imposes — both the physical pain and the psychological terror of not being able to breathe.

Katherine was Rilke's contemporary. She was born when he was twelve and died four years before him, when she was only thirty-four. Both of them were wanderers over Europe, but for different reasons. Heart and lung problems made English winters difficult for her, so she sojourned in southern Italy or France until the British weather moderated. At times she was a patient in Germany, France, Italy, and in Switzerland, not too far from Rilke's Castle Muzot.

Both of them were acquainted with writers in various European countries, and spoke several languages, but from my limited research, I do not think they ever met or were even aware of one another. The only time I can pinpoint that both were resident in the same place is in the early months of 1914, in Paris. Rilke was in a period of dryness and was translating André Gide into German to support himself. He indicates in a letter that he did not go out or see many people, except to consult Gide on doubtful passages.

It was a difficult time for Katherine Mansfield, too. She wrote in her *Journal* one night in February:

> *It is as though God opened his hand and let you dance on it a little, and then shut it up tight— so tight that you could not even cry.*[2]

Had she seen Rodin's "Hand of God"—that hand that seemed to Rilke to be holding us tenderly as we fall? Did it appear to reach out to her to tempt her to dance, only to close and suffocate her?

Rilke wrote: *It stands in me, that house I look for still...*Katherine Mansfield also had a house within. The dream of the permanent home she and John Middleton Murry would have when she regained her health and could live year round in England sustained her through all her wanderings and sufferings and the upheavals of the First World War.

They called this house The Heron Farm, in memory of Katherine's brother Leslie, whose middle name was Heron. There would be a small cottage and they would raise much of their food in the garden. And they would also have a printing press and publish their own writings, and live simply and happily.

Their friends, Leonard and Virginia Woolf, had their own printing press. The publishing house they established, which became Hogarth Press, brought out early editions of some of Katherine's writing. Virginia and Katherine were close friends, but also rivals in their efforts to become established writers.

She was born Kathleen Mansfield Beauchamp, in Wellington, New Zealand, on October 14, 1888. She chose her pen name in college. Katherine seemed more sophisticated than Kathleen, she thought, and her middle name more euphonious than her last. She was Katherine Mansfield to everyone for the rest of her life.

She was the third of five children in a large warm family that included not only her parents and her siblings, but her grandmother and her mother's as-yet-unmarried sister, plus a variety of servants. Her mother had had rheumatic fever and was a semi-invalid. The grandmother ran the household and held the family together with wisdom, love, and common sense. Katherine began writing as a child and her first short story was published when she was nine.

While the children were young, the family moved for a time to a large rambling house in a small community outside Wellington. She has vividly described the move to the new house in her story "Prelude." This house, with its exciting possibilities for hiding places and adventures, becomes familiar to us in story after story, and the family members come to seem like old friends. We have a vivid picture of the children's country school in "The Doll's House."

When she was thirteen, the three eldest children—all girls—were sent to England to complete their education at Queens College in London. Katherine was a bit young, but she was precocious and had finished what education was to be had at home. An older student, Ida Baker, was assigned to welcome the New Zealanders. She acted as a "big sister" to Katherine and they became lifelong friends. Both wanted to be writers and both chose pen names. Ida became Lesley Moore, choosing a name that seemed ambigious as to sex, an advantage to a woman trying to publish. Katherine probably suggested the name, since her brother's name was Leslie. They called one another KM and LM. LM never did become a professional writer, although in 1972, when she was in her 80's, she published her memoirs of Katherine Mansfield. She was utterly devoted to

Katherine all her life and found many ways to relieve her of tiresome and time-consuming details of living and travelling.

Katherine was a music student, majoring in 'cello. She was also a competent pianist. She was a prolific contributor to the college paper and became its editor.

After graduation, the three sisters were fetched back home to New Zealand, Katherine, at least, most reluctantly. She had glimpsed the exciting literary world of London. How could she ever become a writer in the provincial backwaters? Back home she was restless and rebellious and made life miserable for her family. Finally her father gave her a small allowance and let her return to London. He could have provided for her amply, but he reasoned that if the allowance were small, she would have to live simply and stay out of trouble. He was confident she would find that she could not make it and would return home.

She was not about to go home. She found ways to augment her money: she sang in nightclubs, and found walk-on parts in operas and bit parts in movies. All this she viewed as the ''experience'' a writer needs, out of which to write. She did some foolish things and there were people ready to exploit her.

Some of these exploits and exploiters found their way into her stories. She entered into a hasty marriage, but after one night she had had enough and left her husband.

My copy of *Bartlett's Quotations*, the eleventh edition, edited by Christopher Morley, has three lines from a poem she wrote in London when she was nineteen or twenty. She's not a great poet, but I found this one charming. It evokes the memory of two children sleeping together in a big bed and trying to stay awake. One of them falls asleep and the other creeps to the window and watches a flock of sheep passing by in the snow:

> O flock of thoughts with their shepherd Fear
> Shivering, desolate, out in the cold,
> That entered into my heart to fold! [3]

Her calling was not to be a poet, but to write short stories. Gradually she began to publish a few and to gain some recognition. She was experimenting with the plotless, slice-of-life short story, one of the first to try this form, and one of the first to take as her subject ordinary people in everyday situations. And she did make use of her own experience.

John Middleton Murry, still an Oxford undergraduate, was editor of an avant-garde magazine called *Rhythm*, to which she submitted a short story. "The Woman at the Store" tells what a hard life and isolation have done to a woman in the New Zealand bush. Murry was so impressed by the story that he wanted to meet the author. A mutual friend invited them both to dinner, and Murry described the meeting in detail in his autobiography. He was fascinated by her and dwells on how she unconsciously cupped her hand so that it reminded him of a shell. He sensed her authenticity and commented that she made "pretentious people uncomfortable." He was later astonished to find that she was drawn to him and their relationship quickly blossomed into love.

Katherine's husband of one night would not grant her a divorce for a long time, however. He, of course, has his own version of the story. She and Murry were not free to marry until May 1918, by which time they had been living together for six years.

Early in the war, Katherine's brother came to England to enlist. Now reunited as adults, they had a wonderful time remembering together their New Zealand childhood. He was killed in France shortly after their reunion. She wrote in her *Journal*:

> *I do not wish to go anywhere; and the only possible value that anything can have for me is*

*that it should put me in mind of something that
happened or was when he was alive.*

*"Do you remember, Katie?" I hear his
voice...I have a duty to perform to the lovely time
when we were both alive. I want to write about it,
and he wanted me to. We talked it over in my
little top room in London. I said: I will just put on
the front page: To my brother, Leslie Heron
Beauchamp. Very well: it shall be done.*[4]

And it *was* done. The "lovely time when they
were both alive" yielded her best, and best known,
stories. "Prelude," "At the Bay," "The Garden
Party," "The Doll's House," and many others fulfill
her promise to her brother.

An attack of pleurisy in 1914 began the long
struggle with lung problems and the annual journey
to the south of France or Italy. Each year, as the war
advanced, travel became more difficult and the
journeys left her exhausted. Murry was tied to London by his work as editor of various journals, but he
came to be with her when he could get away.

One such time they both looked back on as the
epitome of their happiness. She found a small house,
the Villa Pauline, and he came in December 1915 and
was able to stay three months. It was a golden time.
The weather was beautiful and both of them were in

creative periods. They spent the mornings writing, sitting on opposite sides of the kitchen table. He was writing his book on Dostoyevsky and she was completing her first little book of short stories about her New Zealand childhood. In the afternoons they explored the lovely countryside, and each evening, as a game, they chose a subject and wrote poems on it, or they wrote a joint one.

During the long months of separation, Katherine wrote to Murry every day, and her letters are beautiful reading. He published them after her death. He wrote to her too, and her emotional health and often her physical health seemed to depend on his letters. But distance and the war resulted in irregular delivery and their arrival in bunches. It was a hard way to keep in touch.

Her return journey in the spring of 1918 caught her in Paris during the German offensive and she was stranded there for ten days while the city was bombed. Fortunately, her faithful LM had come to help her make the journey. They camped out in a cheap hotel, eating in restaurants whose supplies were dwindling. Katherine finally gave up the constant trips to the air raid shelter because the dampness aggravated her coughing. There was no transportation, and of course no mail, in or out of the city.

She arrived back in London, a full month after leaving southern France, very ill. Her divorce decree, she discovered, had finally come through at last, and she and Murry were married in May, 1918.

One hesitates to pass judgment on Murry, but it is hard to avoid the conclusion that he often failed to understand her needs and that she felt let down many times. He was a prolific writer, with more than a score of books to his credit, most of them literary criticism and social philosophy. During her lifetime, however, he was hard put to earn enough to support himself, let alone a wife with mounting medical bills. He was a strange, often moody man, given to much introspection and self-doubt. And yet they loved one another and filled basic needs for each other.

She wrote against time, often in acute pain. She left eighty-eight short stories, twenty-six unfinished by her own standards, for there was not time to give them the final polishing and reworking. There was so much interest in her life and work and in her courageous acceptance of her illness and impending death, that afterwards Murry felt he should make available everything she had ever written. He published not only her *Journal* and her letters, but even her jottings and notes to herself, much of it trivial and not good. Some of it is so personal as to seem an intrusion into her privacy, and others' privacy too. Some of it was petty comments about contemporaries who were still living. It is part of the syndrome of advanced tuberculosis that people become petty and over-critical. She knew this and she fought against it. She deserved a more discriminating publishing of her personal writing.

But one cannot regret that Murry published her *Journal*. I keep meeting people whose lives have been touched by its courage, as mine has been. Parts of it came as if personally addressed to me, as I re-read it in the days when I tried to understand and come to terms with my daughter's death. Here is one such passage:

> *I do not want to die without leaving a record of my belief that suffering can be overcome. For I do believe it. What must one do? There is no question of what is called 'passing beyond it.' This is false.*
>
> *One must* submit. *Do not resist. Take it. Be overwhelmed. Accept it fully. Make it part of life. Everything in life that we really accept undergoes a change. So suffering must become Love. This is the mystery. This is what I must do. I must pass from personal love to greater love. I must give to the whole of life what I gave to one....*
> *Here, for a strange reason, rises the figure of*

*Doctor Sorapure. He was a good man. He helped
me not only to bear pain, but he suggested that
perhaps bodily ill-health is necessary, is a repairing process, and he was always telling me to con-
sider how man plays but a part in the history of
the world. My simple kindly doctor was pure of
heart as Tchehov was pure of heart. But for these
ills one is one's own doctor. If 'suffering' is not
a repairing process, I will make it so. I will learn
the lesson it teaches....*

*It is to lose oneself more utterly, to love more
deeply, to feel oneself part of life,—not separate.*

*Oh Life! accept me—make me worthy—
teach me.*

And then she adds:

*I write that. I look up. The leaves move in the
garden, the sky is pale, and I catch myself weeping. It is hard—it is hard to make a good death.*[5]

In the years since the accident I have tested the
validity of her words. This I know out of my experience, as she knew: Pain can be used for repair, for
growth, for transmutation into love. And I know also
that in the end, one must be one's own doctor. The
will to wholeness and to health must come from within us. When we accept our pain, not seeking to dull it
with pain-killers, when we search for the lesson it
has to teach, we have taken the first steps to over-
coming it.

And I know, also, that this is as true for grief as it is for pain. *I must pass from personal love to greater love,* she said. *I must give to the whole of life what I gave to one.* Grief accepted, experienced fully, can be transmuted into compassion. Love given to one daughter must be poured out unstintingly to others: to her siblings, to our foster children, to the children of friends, to George's students, to children playing on the street or passing me on their way to school. And to children I do not see, who are hungry, abandoned, or battered.

And I have had to reach out to other parents in grief, both personally and through my writing. I need to tell them that I understand and care. I need to tell them that we share the human lot. People in all ages have lost daughters, and sons too. They have left records of their grief; they have transmuted it into poetry, music, sculpture. We were not singled out for grief. We are not alone. Pain and grief are implicit in existence. She said in one of her letters to Murry that everything has its shadow.

At times Katherine Mansfield does seem to be writing for the world, not just for herself. This entry in the *Journal* is dated December 15, 1919:

> *...Honesty (why?) is the only thing one seems to prize beyond life, love, death, everything. It*

alone remaineth. O you who come after me, will you believe it? At the end truth *is the only thing* worth having; *it is more thrilling than love, more joyful and more passionate. It simply cannot fail. All else fails. I, at any rate, give the remainder of my life to it and it alone.*

Murry writes in his Introduction to the *Journal*:

"...after the publication of 'Bliss,' she began to receive many letters from simple people who loved her work, and above all, the child Kezia who appeared in it. She felt she had a responsibility to these people. To them she must tell the truth, and nothing but the truth. This preoccupation with truth, in what she told and in herself to be worthy to tell it, became the devouring passion of her last years." [7]

And in another *Journal* entry she wrote:

But the late evening is the time—of times. Then with that unearthly beauty before one it is not hard to realise how far one has to go. To write something that will be worthy of that rising moon, that pale light. To be 'simple' enough, as one would be simple before God... [8]

She seemed to lay on me the necessity of bearing witness to the truth—the truth that I know out of *my* experience. "To this end was I born, and for this cause came I into the world, that I should bear witness unto the truth," as Jesus told Pilate. (John 18:37) For this were we all born. Katherine Mansfield seemed to urge me not to put off doing it, but to get it down on paper. I had been a speaker most of my life, bearing witness to the truth as I saw it, but now I felt the necessity to leave a more permanent record of what I have come to know out of my experience. How else would my grandchildren know the journey I have made?

As I have tried the last half dozen years to make a writer of myself, coping with all the struggles and procrastinations that make up the "writer's syndrome," it has been good to return to the *Journal* from time to time and to find Katherine Mansfield coping with the same problems.

How well I know this condition:

I knelt down by the bed. But I could not pray. I had done no work. I was not in an active state of grace.[9]

And how I sympathize with this:

It is so strange! I am suddenly back again, coming into my room and desiring to write, Knock, goes Miss Chapman at the door. A man has come to clean the windows. I might have known it!

*And so death claims us. I am sure that just at
that final moment a knock will come and Some-
body Else will come to 'clean the windows.'* [10]

So I take myself to the typewriter, day after day,
remembering Katherine, and how early her gift was
extinguished. Would that I could give her some of
my hours!

The *Journal* also records her search for wholeness:

> *I have got more or less used to pain at last. I
> wonder sometimes if this is worse or better than
> what has been; but I don't expect to be without.
> But I have a suspicion—sometimes a certainty—
> that the real cause of my illness is not my lungs at
> all, but something else. And if this were found
> and cured, all the rest would heal.* [11]

So there is one more brief chapter. By the fall of
1922 she had decided to give up medical treatment
and to seek spiritual healing. She decided to join the
Gurdjieff Institute at Fontainebleau in France,
hoping for spiritual rebirth. She made the decision
against the advice and wishes of Murry, of LM, and
of many friends. Just before she left, she wrote in
her *Journal:*

> *Now, Katherine, what do you mean by health?*

And what do you want it for?

Answer: By health I mean the power to live a full, adult, living, breathing life in close contact what I love—the earth and the wonders thereof—the sea—the sun. All that we mean when we speak of the external world. I want to enter into it, to be part of it, to live in it, to learn from it, to lose all that is superficial and acquired in me and to become a conscious, direct human being. I want, by understanding myself, to understand others. I want to be all that I am capable of becoming so that I may be (and here I have stopped and waited and it's no good—there's only one phrase that will do) a child of the sun.[12]

Olgivanna (later Mrs. Frank Lloyd Wright), one of the members of the Gurdjieff community, wrote of Katherine's arrival there:

"She stood in the doorway of our main dining-room and looked at all and at each with sharp, intense, dark eyes. They burned with the desire and hunger for impressions. She wanted to sit down with all the students, but someone called her to a different dining-room. I asked whose that wonderful face was—I did not notice her body. 'She is a writer, an Englishwoman, her name is Katherine Mansfield.' I wanted to know her....

"One of the most humane acts Gurdjieff ever did was to accept her into the Institute.

"I told him what a lovely face she had and how much I liked her. 'You take care of her,' he said. 'Help her all you can.'

"I knocked on the door of her room. She was sitting by the fireplace. Very white face, dark hair cut short, 'bangs' over her forehead, fine nose and mouth, a delicate chin. But the eyes!... She motioned with a very pale, slender hand which opened half way, with the fingers put to gether: a very shy and restrained gesture..."[13]

It was the same hand that had caught Murry's fancy the night they met!

Thinking of the advanced state of her tuberculosis when she went to Fontainebleau, one is horrified at the sheer hardness of the life. She wrote to LM to send her warm underwear. Apparently the only heat was the fireplaces and the rooms were draughty and cold. One is puzzled that someone with a lung disease was assigned to work in the kitchen preparing vegetables, for she wrote LM that her hands were ruined from scraping carrots. After three months, however, she felt she had made great spiritual progress. She wrote to Murry and asked him to visit her, and he came the afternoon of January 9, 1923. He wrote:

"I have never seen, nor shall I ever see, any one so beautiful as she was on that day; it was as though the exquisite perfection which was always hers had taken possession of her completely." [14]

There was a party in the great hall that night. Olgivanna later told LM that Katherine was so full of joy and love that her face was transfigured with beauty. She left the party early to go to her room, and without thinking, apparently, she ran up the stairs, forgetting her weakness. The extra effort resulted in a fit of coughing which culminated in a violent hemmorhage. At 10:30 of the evening Murry had come, she was gone.

The last entry in the *Journal* reads:

I wrote this for myself. I shall now risk sending it to J. He may do with it what he likes. He must see how much I love him.
And when I say 'I fear'—don't let it disturb you, dearest heart. We all fear when we are in waiting-rooms. Yet we must pass beyond them, and if the other can keep calm, it is all the help we can give each other....
And this all sounds very strenuous and ser-

ious. But now that I have wrestled with it, it's no longer so. I feel happy—deep down. All is well. [15]

Yes, all is well! It is useless to regret the unwritten stories, and all that she might have done with length of days. If she had had unlimited expectations, the *Journal* would not speak so deeply to those in pain and grief. Let us celebrate what she did accomplish, amazed that so much was completed and that so much is good and memorable. And let us give thanks for her *Journal*, her witness to the truth, written out of such anguish.

And I came to see that *all is well* with my daughter, too. The "appearance of suffered injustice" that Rilke spoke of began to leave me. I no longer dwell on what she might have done in a normal lifetime. I am quietly, humbly grateful for the twenty-three years we shared life, and proud of all she did accomplish.

And I still keep finding evidence of lives she touched. Fourteen years after her death, George and I spoke at Poughkeepsie Friends Meeting. A woman, perhaps in her late thirties, came to me quietly afterwards, hesitating whether to speak or not. She told me that about twenty years before, she had met Sara at Circle Pines Camp in Michigan one summer and had been impressed by her. They talked long one night about religion, and Sara spoke simply, articulately, and warmly about what it meant to her to be a Friend. At the end of the camp period they went their separate ways. Many years later when she was married and had several children, her husband was transferred to Poughkeepsie. They felt it was time to join a church—but which one? Then she remembered Sara whose life had spoken so deeply to her, and they sought out the Friends Meeting.

All her life Katherine Mansfield read and reread Shakespeare. Her *Journal* and her letters often contain comments on passages in which she found new insights. She is buried at Fontainebleau. On the simple stone is a line from Henry the Fourth (II,iii) which she loved:

> *Out of this nettle, danger, we pluck this flower, safety.*

Grief and pain and finiteness are part of everyone's inner world. There is no way around them. We must find the courage to accept them, so that we can come out on the other side. Even death—like the nettle—loses its sting when grasped with courage. And we find that *all is well.*

> *Everything in life that we really accept undergoes a change. So suffering must become Love....*

Oh life! accept me—make me worthy—teach me.

Rilke wrote,

They've finally no more need of us, the early departed,...

But we, that have need of such mighty secrets, we, for whom sorrow's so often source of blessedest progress, could we exist without them? [16]

Chapter IV

Rabindranath Tagore

"Let it not be a death but completeness."

ABOUT A YEAR before her death, Katherine Mansfield wrote in her *Journal:*

> *Tidied all my papers. Tore up and ruthlessly destroyed much. This is always a great satisfaction. Whenever I prepare for a journey I prepare as though for death. Should I never return, all is in order. This is what life has taught me.* [1]

When we returned home after the accident, George and I were astonished to find to what extent Sara's affairs were in order. She had just completed her second year of a doctoral program and her course notes were all put away neatly in the file by her desk. Another file drawer contained material for her dissertation, for she was working part time at a psychiatric institute and out of her work gathering thesis material. Another file drawer contained the correspondence of the Young Friends of North America of which she was Clerk. The records and the correspondence were all up to date and could be turned over to her successor without delay. Her financial affairs were in good order, her bills paid, check book up to date, and everything neatly in her desk drawer.

True, she was about to embark on a journey to Europe only a few days after the wedding. She was eagerly looking forward to the summer. In no way was she anticipating disaster or thinking she might not return. All during our journey her talk was full of her summer plans and the future directions of her life.

She was well organized by habit, else she could not have accomplished all she did. In addition to the full academic program, the part-time job, the two voice lessons a week, she made most of her own clothes and kept the family supplied with homemade bread.

Her parents, also heavily committed, were rebuked by the state of her affairs. Had either of *us* not returned after the accident, a heavy burden would have fallen on our children. I was grateful that I still had time to deal with things so that a mess would not be left behind should I fail to return home from some journey in the future.

I kept telling myself that I must set my house in order, but the house needs some explanation. When I first went to Chicago in 1936 to be a student at Chicago Theological Seminary, I was astonished to arrive at the address of the women's dormitory to find a most unusual building. It has become famous in the years since, for it is the Robie House, the culmination of Frank Lloyd Wright's prairie period. Thus began our long interest in Wright's architecture. In our early years in Chicago, George and I walked all over the south side, identifying the Wright buildings, and on Sunday afternoons we often rode the double deck bus to locate others in the city.

There was a special house about a mile north of Robie House. We wished we had the courage to knock and ask if we might go through it. A dozen years later when we had three children and were looking for a house to buy, we learned that "our house" —as we had always thought of it—was for sale. The neighborhood was changing and the owner wanted desperately to get out while he could. We had made the decision to buy in the area, if we could, because we wanted to be part of the changes going on there. We wanted to help create a stable interracial community.

A fifteen-room mansion by Frank Lloyd Wright was not exactly what we were looking for when we set out house-hunting, but here was our excuse to see the inside of the house at last. We boldly went along with the real estate agent, as legitimate house-hunters. And that was our downfall, for it was even more wonderful on the inside than on the outside.

We made an offer without any expectation that the owner would accept it. He was, however, so anxious to leave the community that he lowered his price and eventually accepted our offer. And so, incredible as it seemed at the time, that wonderful house became our home for twenty-five years. It made many things possible, including expanding our family to include our four beloved foster daughters. And it brought to us many ''guests of our lives,'' for there was room and to spare to share with many people—from overnight guests to students from other countries whose American home it became.

A fifteen-room house provides, also, space for things to accumulate. And how they did accumulate! Setting the house in order was no simple task. I went back to work too soon after the accident, before I had fully recovered from my own injuries. The house was so full of memories that I could not bear to stay in it day after day. So the years went by, and our big old inner-city house remained as disorganized—and as comfortable and livable—as ever. I was in good health most of the time. I expected to live to a ripe old age. In retirement there would be time to sort things. In spite of the accident, in spite of losing a daughter, I had not yet accepted, not yet internalized *my* own finiteness.

Then, suddenly without warning, six years after the accident, I was struck down by pneumonia. I had never been sick enough to need antibiotics before and now I found that I was allergic to all of them. In my more lucid moments in the hospital, I was aware that I might not survive. I promised myself that if I recovered I would no longer postpone the setting of my house in order. I meant this in every way. I meant it literally — the actual house, all fifteen rooms of it — and I also meant personal habits, relationships, and directions. I found myself praying

> *Only let me make my life simple and straight,*
> *like a flute of reed for thee to fill with music.* [2]

The line is Tagore's. Where had I first glimpsed the possibilities of living in such a way that death would not catch one unprepared? The long weeks of convalescence found me immersed in Rabindranath Tagore.

He was no newcomer to my life; he had long been a guest. When I was only fourteen, I had discovered his little book, *Gitanjali*, one day while browsing in a downtown book store in Cleveland where I grew up. I did not know anything about Tagore, but I knew I had to have that book, and I spent my lunch money for it. It has been part of my life for fifty years.

How often Tagore's words have come to me at some illuminated moment. When my small daughter, Sara, first lay in my arms, not quite forty-five minutes old, I was longing to give her freedom to be herself, and I greeted her with words of Tagore:

*Let my love, like sunlight, surround you
and yet give you illumined freedom.* [3]

And how often, after her death, I read and reread these lines:

In desperate hope I go and search for her in all the corners of my room; I find her not.
My house is small and what once has gone from it can never be regained.
But infinite is thy mansion, my lord, and seeking her I have come to thy door.
I stand under the golden canopy of thine evening sky and I lift my eager eyes to thy face.
I have come to the brink of eternity from which nothing can vanish—no hope, no happiness, no vision of a face seen through tears.
Oh, dip my emptied life into that ocean, plunge it into the deepest fullness. Let me for once feel that lost sweet touch in the allness of the universe. [4]

Tagore seemed the right companion for my long convalescence from pneumonia.

He was a genius of the magnitude of Shakespeare, or Mozart, or Goethe. His talent was early recognized and nurtured, and fame and world-wide honor came to him. He was the first Asian to receive the Nobel Prize for Literature (for *Gitanjali*), in 1913. He was knighted in 1915, but resigned the honor four years later to protest the Amritsar massacre. He travelled widely and was truly a world citizen. He was equally at home discussing land reform with peasants or the nature of reality with Einstein.

He wrote approximately fifty plays, one hundred books of verse, forty novels, much shorter fiction, books of essays, philosophy, and devotional literature. His songs, for which he wrote both words and music, early passed into the folk music of India. Later in life he became a symbolist painter of originality. Whatever he attempted, he did well.

He was born May 6, 1861, in Calcutta, the fourteenth child of his parents. (I'm not sure what that says for family planning!) It was a distinguished family, abounding in artists, poets, and musicians. Growing up with all this creativity, Rabindranath was encouraged to express himself in many media. When guests came, he would be asked to read his poetry and sing his songs. The Tagore name opened many doors for him. By the time he was twenty, he had published several volumes of poetry and a novel, and had had plays produced in Calcutta.

His father was a leader of a new monotheistic movement in Hinduism, known as the Brahma Samaj. This wise and saintly man was always observing his gifted youngest son and thinking: now what does he need next to help him grow and develop his gifts? — and then arranging it.

When Rabindranath was eleven, his father took him along on an extended retreat in the Himalayas. Was it a vacation for the boy? Before the sun rose, they were up for his daily lesson in Sanskrit. After a glass of milk, the father taught him portions of the Upanishads and they chanted them together. At sunrise they went for a walk, then English lessons and a swim. After lunch, more lessons. In the evening they sat on the veranda, chanting devotional hymns, and as the sky darkened the father taught him the rudiments of astronomy.

When he was eighteen, he was sent to England for two years of study, and upon his return his father felt he should take some adult responsibility in a large land-owning family. So he put him in full charge of the family estates, spread over a wide area. His headquarters became a houseboat from which he looked after the family interests and adjusted them as he could to the welfare of the tenants. This gave him his first awareness of the actual daily drudgery of the peasants.

He grew up in an Indian-style extended family. When he was a boy, an older brother took a child bride a year or so older than Rabindranath. The two were often tutored together. He lived in his mother's quarters until she died when he was thirteen. After that his older brother and his sister-in-law included him in their living quarters and in their activities and travels. The playmate of his boyhood became in a very real way a mother figure too, one of the deepest influences of his life.

Then, when she was twenty-five, this beloved sister-in-law took her own life. Tagore struggled with her death. In his Reminiscences he says that this encounter with death was a lifelong one. As time passed and he gained some detachment, he came to see that finiteness is what gives life its beauty. Life is "painted on the vast canvas of death." Death, he came to see, is the natural consequence of being alive, and since it is inevitable, one should prepare for it, and participate in it fully. This theme recurs in his poetry:

> *Peace, my heart, let the time for the parting be sweet.*

Let it not be a death but completeness.
Let love melt into memory and pain into songs.
Let the flight through the sky end in the folding
  of the wings over the nest.
Let the last touch of your hands be gentle like the
  flower of the night.
Stand still, O Beautiful End, for a moment, and
  say your last words in silence.
I bow to you and hold up my lamp to light you on
  your way. [5]

A marriage was arranged for him. His bride, whom he called Nalini, was only nine at the time. She did not have his sister-in-law's gifts, but she was devoted to him and he came to depend on her and to love her deeply. She must not have found it easy to be his wife. On the one hand he wanted to live austerely and economically as a matter of principle and personal discipline, and on the other he wanted his guests entertained lavishly. Nalini became a resourceful cook and was equal to all occasions. She always dressed simply and wore little jewelry. Tagore was aware that he was inconsistent. He felt it was his greatest fault, and yet he suspected that it might be the source of his creativity.

As his own children grew, Tagore began to plan for their education. The Bengali schools at the time were rigid in discipline and Western in content.

Their goal was to prepare for British civil service jobs and the education was quite unrelated to the everyday life and cultural background of most Indians.

Tagore felt that education should arise out of curiosity. Classes should meet outdoors, under the trees, with the children studying nature first hand, beginning with the very grass on which they were sitting. He began to envision a learning community, where students, teachers, and artists-in-residence would live together, share the work of their common life, and learn from one another.

On that Himalayan trip with his father when he was a boy, they had first stopped for a time at a family retreat a hundred miles west of Calcutta. It was called Santiniketan, which means Abode of Peace. His father used it for periods of meditation. They remained there several days and Rabindranath loved the place. Now he asked his father if he might have it for his school.

The new school began in December 1901, with five boys and five teachers, and "the great brotherhood of the trees" as Tagore said. He was determined to keep the tuition low. He sold his house in Calcutta and devoted Nalini sold her dowry jewels. Life at the school was simple and austere, the food vegetarian and not too plentiful. Everyone had to work hard to keep the place clean and functioning. Tagore sought to inculcate a love of outward simplicity and inward truth.

But for all the plainness of the living there was great beauty too. He taught the boys his own beautiful songs, and the days began and ended with music. They celebrated the change of seasons with poetry and music and pageants. There were festivals for the great events of the country year, for tree-planting, for ploughing, for the harvest.

The idea caught on. The original five boys were joined by many more and by girls as well. More and more scholars and artists wanted to join the community. Classes were small, and as he had envisioned, they met under the trees. Sometimes they met *in* the trees, and sometimes they walked. Tagore felt that children learn with the whole body and that it is difficult for them to think sitting down and at attention.

After the First World War, Tagore had another dream—of a university where young people and scholars from many lands and cultures would learn from one another. In such a place they would come to see the futility of war and violence. Visva-Bharati, which means ''world university,'' was established alongside Santiniketan, the school for children.

Tagore had never forgotten the Bengali peasants whose problems had become familiar to him on his father's estates. An Institute of Rural Reconstruction was established at the Santiniketan complex. Students from the World University worked with the peasants to improve the soil and diversify crops, to fix their latrines and cope with the marauding monkeys. Health clinics were started, co-ops promoted, adult education and teacher training programs begun, and crafts and trades taught. Tagore named the Rural Reconstruction Institute Sriniketan, which means Abode of Grace.

With all his creativity, Tagore had the necessary organizational and promotional skills to make his educational dreams a reality. I read much about Santiniketan and Visva-Bharati while I recovered from pneumonia. How right his educational vision seemed!

Meanwhile I was not able to do much about simplifying life and bringing about a right ordering of things. My lungs did not fully heal, and the level of air pollution in Chicago did not help. Many days I could not function, and even on good days, I no longer worked at full capacity. I gave up my job. Reluctantly we opened ourselves to the possibility of leaving Chicago—leaving our wonderful house, our beloved Friends Meeting, our interracial community, and work that we loved. We were both clear that we would rather make a complete break than to try to reconstitute the old life from a new suburban base. Our children were all grown now, the youngest with just one more year of college. The big old house and the professorial income were no longer needed. Was there some new adventure to which we might give the last working years of our lives?

Such is the efficiency of the Quaker grapevine, that we had hardly voiced these thoughts to ourselves, when the opportunity came to go to Friends World College, whose world headquarters are on Long Island. And despite the reservations of our well-meaning friends, this call took hold of us. The College might be beset by problems, being new and experimental, but the dream was right. And it was familiar, for Friends World College is the spiritual descendant of Santiniketan and Visva-Bharati—another embodiment of Tagore's learning community, where education grows out of experience and people of many cultures and faiths live and work and learn together.

Friends World College has centers in North America, Latin America, Europe, the Middle East, Africa, South Asia, and East Asia. Students enter at one of the centers and usually spend the first year on their home continent. At least a year on two other continents is the requirement for graduation. It is a "university without walls," most of the work being in the form of independent study projects. The main faculty activity is the one-to-one advising relationship. Everyone keeps a journal, an in-depth record of experience, reading, thinking, learning. It may also have poetry, art work, photography, weaving, or performance components of music, dance, mime or the like. There is a great deal of student input at all levels, starting with the three-person presidency, one of those persons being a student, chosen by the world-wide community, who takes a leave of absence for a year to serve as a full-time paid executive. The young people who come through the program are clear-eyed, tough-minded, compassionate world citizens, with a great variety of coping skills, and a longing to help heal the world's wounds.

The move to the College inevitably necessitated the drastic simplification of our lives. My parents had lived with us the last years of my father's life. After his death my mother could not face sorting his papers and other things. They were packed away in trunks and cartons to be dealt with later. They joined the trunks filled with my brother's possessions.

He had been killed in the South Pacific during the Second World War. There was plenty of room in the big house for storage, and plenty of time to deal with these things later. After Sara's death I understood why my mother could not face parting with anything connected with my father or my brother. Now I must, of necessity, sort, discard, give away all the things associated with these three beloved guests of my life.

Within a few months we found ourselves moving from Chicago to Huntington, on Long Island, our fifteen-room house replaced by a four-room cottage, and our income shrinking by more than half. The inner city streets we loved gave way to the woods and and fields and shores of Long Island which we love in a different way. As I think about the College's financial struggles, I remember the early struggles of Santiniketan and I take courage.

There was a tangible link with Tagore in our move. In the summer of 1948 George and I led an eight-week International Student Seminar for the American Friends Service Committee. One of our resource people was Amiya Chakravarty, who had been Tagore's literary secretary from 1926 to 1933. He had sometimes stayed with us in Chicago in the intervening years. He is a Trustee of Friends World

College, and has been interested in it for the dozen years the College has been in existence. When he finally retired (for the second time) from his professorship at the State University of New York at New Paltz, he returned to Santiniketan in 1977-78 to be poet-in-residence.

But I have got ahead of Tagore's story. A year after Santiniketan was established, Nalini died at the age of twenty-nine. For two months that fall he had nursed her day and night, staying by her bed, gently fanning her, hour after hour. But there was no time to give way to grief. Soon after his wife's death, the middle one of his five children, a daughter called Rani, was taken very ill. Tagore took her and the two youngest children to the mountains to escape the heat. Even with the care of three children, one of them seriously ill, the poems kept coming. They were all about children and for children and are collected in his book, *The Crescent Moon.* Some of the loveliest ones have been set to music, in their English translations, by John Alden Carpenter and are familiar.

All his lovely poems, all his tender care, all the cool mountain air could not restore Rani to health, and nine months after her mother, she too died. She was thirteen. Four months after that a young man on the school staff, a gifted poet, whom Tagore loved as a son, died of smallpox, and the school had to be closed for a time to prevent an epidemic. In 1905 his revered and dearly loved father died. And two years later, five years after Nalini, his youngest son, Samindranath, died of cholera.

After this overwhelming series of losses, Tagore retreated for a period of solitude. Out of this came the little book by which he is best known to the English-speaking world, *Gitanjali*, which means "song offerings." Tagore learned to offer to God his grief, his loneliness, his work, his days and years, and his finiteness. The art deepened and became universal. The gifted popular writer of the early years became the great mystic poet.

The major translator of Tagore into English is Tagore himself. In Bengali the poetry has rhyme, meter, and other poetic devices, but the English translations are prose, with a suggestion of rhythm. The first dozen years of this century had taken their toll in mind, body and spirit. Tagore felt he needed a change of scene and fresh ideas. In 1912 he made a journey to England. He embarked on the long sea voyage exhausted and did not feel up to any new creative effort. As he lay in his deck chair, day after day, the idea came to translate some of the poems from *Gitanjali* into English, as a gift for the friends he would soon be seeing.

He gave them to his friend William Rothenstein, an artist who had spent some time in India and who had made some beautiful portraits of Tagore. Excited by the gift, Rothenstein showed them to William Butler Yeats, the great Irish poet, who undertook to have them published and who wrote the moving preface. Yeats wrote:

> "These lyrics—which are in the original, my Indians tell me, full of subtlety of rhythm, of untranslatable delicacies of colour, of metrical invention—display in their thought a world I have dreamed of all my life long. The work of a supreme culture, they yet appear as much the growth of the common soil as the grass and the rushes . . .
>
> "A whole people, a whole civilization, immeasurably strange to us, seems to have been taken up into this imagination; and yet we are not moved because of its strangeness, but because we have met our own image."[6]

His words reflected my own experience even as a girl. And still, after fifty years, Tagore's words move me. His phrases are part of the familiar furniture of my mind and spirit. In this little book are lines to help me center down in meditation, words to repeat when the pressure of time closes in on me, words from which to draw strength and renewal when my heart is dried up, words to help me sleep when sleep eludes me, and above all, words to give expression to my sense of wonder and my joy in created things.

Thou art the sky and thou art the nest as well.
O thou beautiful, there in the nest it is thy love that encloses the soul with colours and sounds and odours.
There comes the morning with the golden basket in her right hand bearing the wreath of beauty, silently to crown the earth.
And there comes the evening over the lonely meadows deserted by herds, through trackless paths, carrying cool draughts of peace in her golden pitcher from the western ocean of rest.
But there, where spreads the infinite sky for the soul to take her flight in, reigns the stainless white radiance. There is no day nor night, nor form nor colour, and never, never a word. [7]

"O thou beautiful" has become my personal mantram.

In that same international student seminar where we met Amiya Chakravarty, one rainy morning during our meditation I was moved to speak lines from

Gitanjali expressing the heart's longing for God:

> *In the deep shadows of the rainy July, with secret steps, thou walkest, silent as night, eluding all watchers.*
>
> *To-day the morning has closed its eyes, heedless of the insistent calls of the loud east wind, and a thick veil has been drawn over the ever-wakeful blue sky.*
>
> *The woodlands have hushed their songs, and doors are all shut at every house. Thou art the solitary wayfarer in this deserted street. Oh my only friend, my best beloved, the gates are open in my house—do not pass by like a dream.*[8]

At the end of our meditation, a young Indian, Baidya Nath Varma, came across the circle to me with shining eyes, incredulous. He pulled from his pocket his own *Gitanjali*, in Bengali. We spent hours that summer reading Tagore together and through him I glimpsed something of the great beauty of these poems in their own language.

In the last years of his life, Tagore travelled widely, exchanging ideas with people and building support for his world university. He visited Japan and wrote enough haikus and other short poems to be collected into two books, *Stray Birds* and *Fireflies*. (The very names of his books are poems!)

In *Stray Birds* is this little nine-word poem:

Be still, my heart, these great trees are prayers.

In her beautiful little book, *The World in Tune*, Elizabeth Gray Vining comments:

"I think I know the very trees that Tagore had in mind when he wrote this, for many of the poems in his volume, *Stray Birds*, were said to have been written at the place in Karuizawa where I spent the summer holidays during my four years in Japan. The house was surrounded by great balsam trees, and the clear pure mountain air was tangy with their fragrance. In the early mornings long shafts of sunlight came slanting through their purplish trunks and green branches, and cuckoos called in the distance. In the hush and freshness, one's heart was filled with that wonder and awe which come when nature silences us with beauty like a trumpet call. Something more explicit than words, higher than thought, deeper than feeling, seemed to be expressed by those majestic trees, as if they were indeed prayer made visible." [10]

Tagore lived to be eighty, and his mind was clear and creative to the end. When he could no longer hold a pen, he dictated poems. There was a memorable eightieth birthday celebration in May 1941, for which he wrote a speech. However, during the summer months his strength failed and he was taken from Santiniketan to Calcutta for an operation. He died on August 7th in the house where he was born.

I have got my leave. Bid me farewell, my brothers! I bow to you all and take my departure.

Here I give back the keys of my door—and I give up all claims to my house. I only ask for last kind words from you.

We were neighbours for long, but I received more than I could give. Now the day has dawned and the lamp that lit my dark corner is out. A summons has come and I am ready for my journey. [11]

"Let it not be a death but completeness," he had written.

On the day when death will knock at thy door what wilt thou offer to him?

Oh, I will set before my guest the full vessel of my life—I will never let him go with empty hands.

All the sweet vintage of all my autumn days and summer nights, all the earnings and gleanings of my busy life will I place before him at the close of my days when death will knock at my door. [12]

I have been learning, with Tagore's help, that when we accept our finiteness realistically and without bitterness, each day is a gift to be cherished and savored. Each day becomes a miracle. I am learning to offer to God my days and my nights, my joy, my work, my pain, and my grief. I am striving to keep my house in order, and my relationships intact. I am learning to use the time I have more wisely, so that death will not catch me with too much undone, too many projects incomplete. But I am learning to work without fretting, and I am finding a sense that there is time "for every purpose under heaven."

And I am learning to forget at times my puritan conscience which prods me to work without ceasing, and instead to take time for joy. I am most fortunate. I have been a city person most of my life — and I love the city. Now, by chance, I live in a beautiful place, remote from the noise and dirt of the city — with water, and trees, and birds, and wild flowers at my door. Walking with George along the shore at dawn, watching the Canada geese who make their home on the pond outside our bedroom window, identifying the wild birds and the wild flowers around us are part of my days, as is keeping an open door for the young people of the campus. (One of them made me a beautiful sign with a wreath of flowers and the words

"Writer at work" to hang on my door when I am not to be disturbed.)

> *Thou hast made me endless, such is thy pleasure. This frail vessel thou emptiest again and again, and fillest it ever with fresh life.*
> *This little flute of a reed thou hast carried over hills and dales, and hast breathed through it melodies eternally new...*
> *Thy infinite gifts come to me only on these very small hands. Ages pass, and still thou pourest, and still there is room to fill.* [13]

And as I think of Tagore's hands into which were poured such infinite gifts, I am reminded once more of Emily Dickinson's hands:

> *For Occupation—This—*
> *The spreading wide my narrow Hands*
> *To gather Paradise—*

Like Tagore's little reed flute, carried over hills and dales, I have carried his little book with me for half a century, and found its songs eternally fresh.

More than thirty years ago a dear Indian friend, George's colleague at Roosevelt University, wrote these lines in our guestbook from memory:

> *Guests of my life,*
> *You came in the early dawn, and you in the night.*

Your name was uttered by the Spring flowers
and yours by the showers of rain.
You brought the harp into my house and you
brought the lamp.
After you had taken your leave I found God's
footprints on my floor.

Here he stopped writing, and for years I assumed that was all of the poem. Now I have learned that there is a final line:

Now when I am at the end of my pilgrimage I
leave in the evening flowers of worship
my salutations to you all. [14]

So now, near the end of my own pilgrimage, I record my gratitude and offer my salutation. Tagore was the great guest who came in the dawn of my life, and who came again in my night. He brought his harp into my house and set my world to music, and his lamp has lightened my darkness. Through him I keep finding God's footprints on my floor.

Chapter V

Alan Paton

"For You Departed"

ONE OF THE POEMS in Tagore's *Gitanjali* is a prayer for his country:

Where the mind is without fear and the head is held high;
Where knowledge is free;
Where the world has not been broken up into fragments by narrow domestic walls;
Where words come out from the depth of truth;
Where tireless striving stretches its arms toward perfection;
Where the clear stream of reason has not lost its way into the dreary desert sand of dead habit;
Where the mind is led forward by thee into ever-widening thought and action—
Into that heaven of freedom, my Father, let my country awake. [1]

Beside that I would like to place this prayer of Alan Paton, who also comes from a troubled land:

Make me, O Lord, the instrument of Thy love, that I may bring comfort to those who sorrow and joy to those who are regarded as persons of little account. In this country of many races make me courteous to those who are humble and understanding to those who are resentful. Teach me

*what I should be to the arrogant and cruel, for I
do not know.*

*And as for me myself, make me more joyful
than I am, especially if this is needed for the sake
of others. Let me remember my many experiences of joy and thankfulness, especially those
that endure. And may I this coming day do some
work of peace for Thee.* [2]

All the other "guests of my life" in this book
were called to be writers—to be poets or story tel-
lers. Alan Paton's calling was to cry out against injustice, and to try to change society. The others
wrote for writing's sake. Out of their personal problems they came to insights that they needed to share
in words. For Paton, writing is both an art and a tool
to rouse people to act. He writes out of full involvement in the struggle for human dignity in his country.

I have long identified with him. Like Paton, I was
confronted by racial injustice when I was young. I
had a friend of another race who was discriminated
against, and I longed to remove the prejudice against
her and against all other human beings arbitrarily
denied full personhood. For thirty-five years in Chicago my primary concern was the struggle for civil
rights and equal opportunities for all people. I
worked both as a volunteer and professionally for
organizations concerned with racial justice. This

commitment underlay all the major decisions George and I made: where we would live, where we would be employed, where we would spend our money, and to what we would give the major portion of our time and energy. Alan Paton's courage, integrity, and steadfastness in defeat always challenged me to make my life, and my witness, and my work more effective.

He came to me as a familiar, but unexpected, guest toward the end of my period of grief. He came in his beautiful little book written in memory of his wife, which he calls *For You Departed*. In it he shares the story of their life together, and I came to appreciate not only the Paton of the novels and the struggle for racial justice, but the private person. His life moves me deeply.

He was born January 11, 1903, in Pietermaritzburg in Natal, still at that time a British colony. When he was seven, two British colonies and two Boer republics united to form the Union of South Africa. The resulting new country has five distinct groups of people. The largest, indigenous, call themselves Africans. The English-speaking call themselves South Africans. The Boers, of Dutch ancestry, call themselves Afrikaners. There is also a large group of Asians, mostly Indian, and in addition, a racially mixed group, called Cape Coloured.

The Patons belong to the English-speaking group. Alan's father, an immigrant from Scotland, was a civil servant; his mother had been a teacher before her marriage. They were Christadelphians— devout, strict, with a deep sense of righteousness which included seeing all people as God's children. Like Emily Dickinson, Alan Paton never joined the family church, but he never lost the sense of righteousness. When he married he joined the Episcopal church which was dear to his wife. His writing reflects how deeply its beautiful liturgy became part of his life. His parents, however, were shocked by the worldliness of Episcopalians, who smoked, and danced and otherwise "sinned."

He graduated with honors in physics from Natal University, having made quite a literary splash as a student with contributions of poetry, plays, and fiction to the university publications. In 1924 the student body chose him to represent them at the first student conference of the British Empire, held in England. After the conference he toured Scotland on a motorcycle. When he returned home he took the Higher Education Diploma to qualify for high school teaching.

His first job was teaching mathematics at a high school in Ixopo in Natal. He had lived in the city most of his life and now he fell in love with the beautiful countryside. He met the woman who was to become his wife on the tennis court in Ixopo. Doris was six years older than he, and married to a man who had tuberculosis. She invited Alan to dinner to meet her sister who was not yet married, but nothing came of the meeting. Her husband guessed intuitively that Paton was in love with Doris.

Though her husband died later that year, they waited three years to marry. They have two sons, David and Jonathan.

It is hard to remember now that there was a time in South Africa before "apartheid," for that policy has been in effect now for so many years. Earlier in this century, however, South Africa had a great political statesman, Jan Smuts. He was a man of brilliance, world-wide influence, and charisma, who was also well known as a philosopher. He was active in the founding of the United Nations and in the framing of its charter. He was, however, not always consistent in his views and actions. At home his political career was often marked by expediency and compromise.

From college days on, Alan Paton was actively involved in a program of summer camps for underprivileged boys. Through this activity he came to know Jan Hofmeyr, for whom the camps were also a life-long interest. Jan Hofmeyr was an Afrikaner, a brilliant and capable man. He became a university president while still in his twenties and then gave that up to enter politics. Paton wrote a biography of his friend after his death which he called *South African Tragedy*. Hofmeyr had been a child prodigy, pushed by a domineering mother. While still in knee pants he went to Oxford to complete his education, his mother going to England with him. He was never able to break away from her. They lived together and took all their vacations together. His adversaries felt that she dominated even his political decisions.

In 1934 Prime Minister Smuts appointed Hofmeyr Minister of Education. Responsibility for the reformatories was transferred from the Department of Prisons to the Department of Education. Hofmeyr wanted to change the grim, punitive institutions into modern training schools.

Alan Paton was ill that year with typhoid fever. During his long convalescence he reflected on the direction of his life. He loved teaching; he had had promotions and was in line for another. He would probably be a headmaster by the time he was fifty. They had a comfortable home, a warm circle of friends, and a pleasant life. But he knew of Hofmeyr's hopes for the reformatories and he decided to apply for the principalship of one of them.

Hofmeyr assigned his friend to the one with the most problems—Diepkloof, at Johannesburg. Paton made the decision in the solitude of his illness. Doris agreed most reluctantly and hoped in vain that it would not be Diepkloof, not Johannesburg. How could they take their small sons to such a place? But as she became involved in the changes he was making, and came to know the new staff he was hiring, her fears disappeared and the once forbidding place became home.

Hofmeyr gave Paton a free hand. He used physical freedom as the prime reward, and proved to his own satisfaction that physical punishment had no effect on the number of offenses committed. Paton became known as the man who pulled up the barbed wire and planted geraniums.

He has written a moving book of short stories called *Tales from a Troubled Land*. Many of them are in the first person and describe incidents of these years. Among them are poignant stories of children and young men to whom death, often violent death, came early, cutting off their lives with no chance of happiness or fulfillment. I weep when I read them.

In 1946 he took a year's leave to study how other

countries were handling corrections, and visited Scandinavia, England, and North America. In September that year he took a train from Stockholm over the mountains into Norway to Trondheim. No one at the desk of the hotel in Trondheim spoke English, so the engineer came up to translate. Then he asked Paton if he would like to see the cathedral. And they sat together looking up at the rose window for a long time. Paton writes:

> *We returned to the hotel about six o'clock, and the engineer said,* I'll call for you at seven, to take you out to dinner. *And I sat there in my room, and out of my homesickness I wrote those words,* there is a lovely road that runs from Ixopo into the hills. [3]

These are, of course, the opening words of *Cry, the Beloved Country*. He finished the manuscript in San Francisco three months later, and shared it with friends who had it typed and undertook to find a publisher. It first appeared in the United States.

What makes this book not only popular in the best-seller sense, but great in the classic sense? I think it is the language, which is beautiful in the way the King James version of the Bible or the Episcopal liturgy is beautiful, as in this passage from Chapter 12, which gives the book its name:

Cry the beloved country, for the unborn child that is the inheritor of our fear. Let him not love the earth too deeply. Let him not laugh too gladly when the water runs through his fingers, nor stand too silent when the setting sun makes red the veld with fire. Let him not be too moved when the birds of his land are singing, nor give too much of his heart to a mountain or a valley. For fear will rob him of all if he gives too much. [4]

In addition, Paton has listened with love to the various languages of his country. As a young man he learned both Afrikaans and Zulu. He reproduces in English the idioms and thought patterns in the speech of the different people in the book. They tell their stories and their language reveals their background, education, and something of their personality.

The book employs many devices. Sometimes he has voices outside the action speak in comment, like a Greek chorus:

All roads lead to Johannesburg. If you are white or if you are black they lead to Johannesburg. If the crops fail, there is work in Johannesburg. If there are taxes to be paid, there is work in Johannesburg. If the farm is too small to be divided further, some must go to Johannesburg. If there is a child to be born that must be delivered in secret, it can be delivered in Johannesburg. [5]

The book changed their lives. As Paton says, "It opened the doors of the world to us, and we went through."[6]

It was well that it was so. In 1948 the Nationalist Party with its policy of apartheid came to power. Smuts was out, and Hofmeyr, his deputy and in line to succeed him when he retired, was, of course, also out. Hofmeyr died that same year in December, when he was only fifty-four. Smuts, an old man, died two years later.

The new minister of Native Affairs closed Diepkloof and dispersed the boys to segregated labor camps. All Paton had accomplished went down the drain—at the same time that he became a world celebrity. Paton turned to writing as a career, and they went to live in an idyllic place on the ocean. However, the volume of correspondence and the constant stream of visitors left no time for writing. (Emily Dickinson could have told him!)

During those five years by the sea he wrote three books, but he had to go away from home and into seclusion to write them. *Too Late the Phalarope*, his second novel, was written in Cornwall. It may be a better novel than the first, but it did not have as wide an appeal. In it he undertakes to portray the thinking and emotions of Afrikaaners. It is a simple story of a young police officer who had been a football hero and war hero, but who transgresses the Immorality Act which forbids sexual relations between members of different races, and thereby brings disaster to his whole family.

Cry, the Beloved Country ends on a note of hope, but there is no hope at the end of *Too Late the Phalarope*. In the five years between the writing of the two books, the political situation altered drastically for the worse.

The Patons were drawn back into the world. First they spent a year at a new tuberculosis settlement, a project of the same organization that ran the camps for boys. They helped to build accommodations for the six hundred patients, to establish gardens, and later to help set up classes to teach skills and trades so that the patients might support themselves when they returned to their homes.

The Liberal Party was founded that year. Alan Paton was elected vice chairman and the following year he became chairman. The Party started a liberal journal, advocating that South Africa open the doors of its society to everyone. Paton wrote a column called "The Long View"—until the government suppressed the publication.

Those who founded the Party could not foresee

that it would arouse the anger of the Nationalists and so result in more restrictive legislation. Its leaders were sometimes arrested and imprisoned without trial. Their movements were restricted, and they could not even participate in social gatherings such as dinner parties. Some of them were "banned." Eventually they were excluded from some occupations and many took exit permits and left the country. Paton's passport was confiscated for a time and he was subjected to a long period of harrassment, with sudden searches, house arrest, and other indignities. He is too much a world figure, however, for the government to restrict his travel indefinitely.

Where did he get his non-racial attitudes? The roots were in his childhood and his family's devout, if narrow, Christianity. He was also influenced by Jan Smuts. Smuts' book, *Holism and Evolution*, made a deep impression on me when I read it for a graduate course in theology at the University of Chicago. He coined the words "holism" and "holistic" which have come into general use. Smuts thought he detected a tendency in the universe pulling everything into larger aggregates, a movement toward synthesis and wholeness.

Paton saw this process happening in his lifetime to himself. He was born into an English-speaking family, and in young manhood became interested in the Afrikaners and their struggle to maintain their language and culture. Later he came to sympathize with the needs and aspirations of the African and Indian people in South Africa, and eventually he felt himself to be a citizen of the world. He has been much more consistent than Smuts himself in living out the implications of the theory of holism which Smuts so persuasively developed.

At the funeral of a friend, Paton had a vision of what a non-racial society would be like. Edith Rheinallt Jones had had a long interest in scouting and for years went into remote places to visit troops of African school girls. During her visits she talked with the tribal chiefs, to health authorities and other government officials, sharing her concerns and suggestions for improving the quality of life. She was known and trusted by black and white people alike.

She had been a staunch supporter of Paton's work at Diepkloof. As she grew older and heavier, she developed a heart condition. Paton used to drive her on her rounds in these later years. And then she died. Paton described her funeral in "The Long View." People of every color and every religion had come together to honor her memory and to give thanks for her life. She had seen each one of them as a friend, and she had made them feel loved and appreciated. She had felt their lives and their work were important and meaningful. Here at her funeral they forgot their fears, their mistrusts, their prejudices. It became for Paton a vision of what South Africa could be like.

Alan Paton gave Arthur Jarvis such a funeral in *Cry, the Beloved Country*. And years later there was such a gathering at the service for Doris Paton. And I noted with interest that it was Paton who gave the eulogy at the funeral of Chief Albert Luthuli, the Nobel Peace Prize winner.

But where did he find the strength to stand steadfast in defeat? He says he found it in St. Francis. He has written a beautiful little book of meditations on the prayer of St. Francis, called *Instrument of Thy Peace*. He wrote it, he says, "for sinners," and for people inclined to be melancholy. It is a book to live with, and I turn to it often.

An American visited him and commented that Paton was not like the man of Christian joy he had expected. (It is true; I have yet to see a picture of Alan Paton smiling, nor have I seen him smile during the television interviews I have watched.) Paton responded that forces beyond his control made conditions in South Africa grave and depressing, and brought personal frustrations. He writes:

> This year a friend of mine wished me a happy
> Easter, and I, because my wife was gravely ill,
> replied that I did not think it would be happy.
> When he reached home, he sat down and wrote to
> me that no Christian should be unhappy at Easter
> because what happened at Easter was of an eter-
> nal order, whereas our griefs were temporal.

> I replied to him that I did not expect to be un-
> happy at Easter. I was prepared to face the future
> and whatever it might bring. I wrote: 'I like to see
> happiness and to see happy people, especially
> happy children. I hope they may grow up happy
> also, but if I had to choose, I would rather see
> them brave.' [7]

Doris Paton was a heavy smoker. She died of lung
cancer, after a long and heartbreaking struggle, in
October 1967. Alan Paton addresses her directly
throughout his memoir, *For You Departed:*

> To you, wherever you are and in whatever
> condition, I send thanks for all your faith and
> courage, for all your help and encouragement,
> for all that strength of character that conquered
> your fears and that clearness of mind that could
> tell a cruel deed in spite of all its wrappings in
> noble words. [8]

I reread the little book that last spring in Chicago,
finishing it just before the crowded weeks of clearing

out the big house for the move to Long Island.

I was clear that it was right for us to go. I was excited by the possibilities of new life at Friends World College and full of confidence that my lungs would heal in the more rural setting, a confidence that was justified. But there was something that troubled both George and me. We had scattered Sara's ashes in the garden, and both of us had a sense of her presence there. How could we go off and leave her and abandon the garden to strangers?

We talked for a while of having some small, inconspicuous plaque made to attach to the wall of the garden. In the end, however, we knew it was not right to lay our grief on the new owners of the house.

I understood then, for the first time, why people need to erect monuments and mark graves. I suspect that the need is as old as human history. In Genesis we read of Rachel's death after she had given birth to Benjamin:

> "And Rachel died, and was buried in the way to Ephrath, which is Bethlehem.
> "And Jacob set a pillar upon her grave: that is the pillar of Rachel's grave unto this day." (Genesis 35: 19-20)

Whether Rachel's pillar exists unto *our* day, I do

not know. But her real monument is the story in Genesis. Across the centuries Rachel leads her sheep to the well and there encounters the eager stranger who rolls the stone away that the sheep may drink. What more beautiful memorial could she have than this:

> "And Jacob served seven years for Rachel; and they seemed unto him but a few days, for the love he had to her." (Genesis 29:20)

Jacob needed to set up his pillar to mark the place where Rachel's beloved body was buried. His caravan was in transit, and he could not remain in the wilderness. He had to move on with all his company.

And we cannot spend the rest of our lives sitting by the graves of those we love. The final stage of grief, I believe, is the creation of a memorial so that we can move on to other things. We must let our beloved dead go, and we must ask them to release us.

But a memorial may take many forms. It may be a poem, or a symphony, or a carving, or a portrait. It may be working as a volunteer in a hospital, or endowing a school, or caring for foster children. Or it may be a memoir, such as Alan Paton wrote for his Doris.

And so in the years since we left Chicago I have been writing of Sara and collecting her poetry and her letters to share with her wider family and her friends. And it seemed good, also, to write in tribute of the "guests of my life" who had shared my pilgrimage through grief.

Alan Paton's book was first published in England under the title *Kontakion*. In the Greek Orthodox Church a *kontakion* is a hymn honoring a saint. On the final page of his book, Paton writes:

> *Something within me is waking from long sleep, and I want to live and move again. Some zest is returning to me, some immense gratefulness for those who love me, some strong wish to love them also. I am full of thanks for life. I have not told myself to be thankful, I just am so.*
>
> *And the book is done too, this Kontakion for you departed. I am glad it came to be written. It has in some strange way refined some dross out of me. It has taught me—though this was not my first lesson—to accept the joys and vicissitudes of life, and to fall in love again with its strangeness and beauty and terror. I have set down here my green and foolish hurts in those days when you loved and tormented me, and I shall never shrink from them again. As I wrote earlier, it is a strange story, and now it is done.*
>
> *I have made my song, alleluya.* [9]

I too found something waking within me. I turned with eagerness to the new life, the new work, the new friends. I am blessed now to live on a college campus among young people only a little younger than Sara was on that June day when we turned homeward from her brother's wedding. In loving them, I am loving her. I give thanks daily for their courage, their joy, their grace, their caring. Truly they are the hope of the world.

And I have learned that no one piece of earth, however hallowed by our memories, is more holy than another. It is all holy. Alleluya!

Chapter VI

Walt Whitman

"...a child went forth..."

ALAN PATON WROTE that he liked to see happy children, and hoped that they would grow up happy, but that if he had to choose, he would rather see them brave.

In wanting the freedom to be herself as my primary gift to my daughter, I was wishing for her not only the happiness of fulfillment, but the courage to achieve it. Like Paton, if I had to choose, I would rather see my children brave if they cannot be both brave and happy, although it was not always easy for me to maintain such an attitude.

Sara went forth with confidence and anticipation—from her first day at nursery school, to the times on Antioch College job periods when we put her on planes bound for cities she had never visited. As we watched her and her siblings grow in self-confidence and competence, we found ourselves becoming more open to possibilities and risks. We came to feel that the unadventurous, nay-saying, security-seeking life is not worth living.

And so, some eight years after Sara's death, we felt that we should leave Chicago—leave the security of a comfortable home, a supportive community of friends, and a tenured professorship, for a new life on Long Island. "Tomorrow to fresh woods, and pastures new," as Milton ended his elegy for Lycidas.

Time and distance have now made it possible for me to write of events that were heartbreaking and terribly personal when they happened. I have come to the place where I can remember without tears. I have found perspective to understand and articulate the long journey through grief, and I have needed to reach out to share my insights with other people.

In some ways life has seemed to come full circle for me here. I have become conscious of the heritage that predisposed me throughout my life, both on the heights as well as in the depths, to turn to poets and storytellers for insights that would lead to self-understanding and for guideposts into the future. Unforeseen at the time we made the decision to come to Long Island, someone was waiting for me, waiting for me to be a guest in his house.

One cannot be very long in Huntington, New York, without knowing whose town this is. Walt Whitman Road, Walt Whitman High School, Walt Whitman Mall, Real Estate, Savings and Loan, Florist, Fish and Lobster Company—you name it, and you will find his name attached. As soon as we had unpacked the books, I began to reread *Leaves of Grass*. I discovered that the poetry that had always seemed so universal was also specifically Long Island in its details.

But Walt Whitman does not live in the enterprises that have appropriated his name. He lives in the house his father built, and he waited for me there. Some months after we came to Huntington, I was asked to work at the Whitman Birthplace.

It is now a New York historic site, an old house on a quiet acre of land, with a busy highway running beside it, and the huge Walt Whitman Mall across the road. Busloads of school children, scout troops, college English classes, scholars, poetry lovers of all ages and many countries, families on rainy Sunday afternoons, the curious and the bored tramp through the house or linger over the displays of *Whitmaniana*. My job was to evoke ''the Whitman presence'' for each of them, if I could. And the job was a joy, for I soon discovered that Whitman is *alive and well* — his phrase — and that he still lives in the house where he was born.

It is a fine old house, cedar-shingled like so many Long Island homes, with hand-fashioned beams held together by wooden pegs, and unusually large windows all around. Whitman's father — for whom the poet was named—had built this house with love, for it was here that he brought his bride, Louisa van Velsor of Cold Spring Harbor. Walt was the second child to be born in the big bed in "the borning room" behind the parlor.

Photographs of Walter and Louisa Whitman hang in the house. I stand and look at them "long and long."

> His own parents, he that had father'd him
>   and she that had conceiv'd him in her
>   womb and birth'd him,
> They gave this child more of themselves
>   than that,
> They gave him afterward every day, they
>   became part of him.
> The mother at home quietly placing the
>   dishes on the suppertable,
> The mother with mild words, clean her cap
>   and gown, a wholesome odor falling off
>   her person and clothes as she walks by,... [1]

Louisa Whitman had come from a Quaker family. She had little formal education, but she was a good manager—cheerful, placid, adjusting to the many changes in her life, before the long discouraging years made her something of a complainer.

The father, strong, self-sufficient, manly,
    mean, anger'd, unjust,
The blow, the quick loud word, the tight
    bargain, the crafty lure,... [2]

Walter Whitman was an unhappy man, often moody
and depressed—a good carpenter, judging from this
house, but a poor businessman, never able to make a
sufficient living for his family.

The first child of the marriage was difficult, perhaps mentally ill or retarded. Louisa really rejoiced
in her second son—sturdy, bright, outgoing, curious
Walt. She imparted to him her Quaker faith in the
goodness, the Light, inherent in everyone—especially himself.

There was a child went forth every day,
And the first object he look'd upon, that object
    he became,
And that object became part of him for the day
    or a certain part of the day,
Or for many years or stretching cycles of years.

The early lilacs became part of this child,
And grass... [3]

as the poetry of the man bears witness. The lilacs still
bloom in "fifth month" in the dooryard of his house,
and the grass spreads green. My first spring on Long
Island I also found the "white and red morning

glories'' growing wild in a field near my home. And

The horizon's edge, the flying sea-crow, the fragrance of salt marsh and shore mud,... [4]

have now become part of my life, as they became part of that child who went forth every day.

A mockingbird became part of this child for stretching cycles of years, as he tells in one of his loveliest poems:

Up this seashore in some briers,
Two feather'd guests from Alabama, two to-
gether,
And their nest, and four light-green eggs spotted
with brown,
And every day the he-bird to and fro near at hand,
And every day the she-bird crouch'd on her nest,
silent, with bright eyes,
And every day I, a curious boy, never too close,
never disturbing them,
Cautiously peering, absorbing, translating. [5]

Then one day the she-bird was gone from the nest, ''maybe killed,'' and day after day and night after night the boy heard the lonely he-bird calling his mate:

O you singer solitary, singing by yourself,
projecting me,

*O solitary me listening, never more shall I cease
    perpetuating you,
Never more shall I escape, never more the
    reverberations,
Never more the cries of unsatisfied love be
    absent from me,
Never again leave me to be the peaceful child
    I was before what there in the night,
By the sea under the yellow and sagging moon,
The messenger there arous'd, the fire, the sweet
    hell within,
The unknown want, the destiny of me.*[6]

Walter Whitman's affairs did not prosper here in Huntington. He decided to try his fortunes in Brooklyn, the big city on the western end of the Island, and they left the shingled house while Walt was still quite small:

*Men and women crowding fast in the
    streets,...
The streets themselves and the facades
    of houses, and goods in the windows,
Vehicles, teams, the heavy-plank'd wharves,
    the huge crossing at the ferries,...*[7]

all these now became part of the child.

But still the family fortunes did not improve. When Walt was eleven, he left school, probably not too unhappy to be through with his formal education.

He went forth to find a job to help support the growing family. In time he apprenticed himself to a newspaper office where he learned to set type and absorbed all the facets of the newspaper game. And he went forth to the library, to museums, to lectures and concerts, continuing his education on his own. His curiosity made him a lifelong learner. The poetry was written by a well-educated man, conversant with all the areas of human knowledge in the nineteenth century.

So a young man grew in Brooklyn, learning to express himself in words, finding out about the world, and coming to love the beauty and vitality of the ordinary, hard-working people whom he met in the streets, in the shops, on the ferries and in the taverns of this exciting young city.

And a book grew in Brooklyn, with strange, unconventional poetry—much of it on themes his fellow citizens did not think fit for polite conversation, and couched in shocking language. Brashly the young man sent a copy to Emerson, who immediately recognized something new and great, writing back by return mail. So what did it matter what others thought?

Scholars speculate on where the poetry came from, for nothing in Whitman's early writing suggests the originality, and the skill and the sureness of *Leaves of Grass*. He was an adequate, but not distinguished journalist.

The poetry apparently grew out of an overwhelming mystical experience Whitman had when he was about thirty. He suddenly sensed the wholeness of the universe as he was looking at a leaf of grass. And he perceived the beauty of all created things, including the human body, and the holiness of love in all its manifestations. To some degree this experience persisted in him for the remainder of his life, a "cosmic consciousness," as Dr. R.M. Bucke, his friend and biographer, called it.

Whitman recounts this mystical experience in his long poem, *Song of Myself*:

> *I loafe and invite my soul,*
> *I lean and loafe at my ease observing a spear of*
> *summer grass....*
> *Swiftly arose and spread around me the peace*
> *and knowledge that pass all the argument*
> *of the earth,*
> *And I know that the hand of God is the promise*
> *of my own,*
> *And I know that the spirit of God is the brother*
> *of my own,*
> *And that all the men ever born are also my broth-*
> *ers, and the women my sisters and lovers,*
> *And that a kelson of the creation is love,...* [8]

And he also saw the oneness of life and death, death being but the eternal recycling of life:

> *What do you think has become of the young and*
> * old men?*
> *And what do you think has become of the women*
> * and children?*
>
> *They are alive and well somewhere,*
> *The smallest sprout shows there is really no*
> * death,*
> *And if ever there was it led forward life, and does*
> * not wait at the end to arrest it,*
> *And ceas'd the moment life appear'd.*
> *All goes onward and outward, nothing collapses,*
> *And to die is different from what any one sup-*
> * poses, and luckier.* [9]

Whitman was in his forties when the Civil War broke out, too old to serve in the Union army. His brother George enlisted. In December 1862, in the office of the *New York Herald*, Walt took a dispatch from the telegraph, and found his brother's name on a list of the wounded in the battle of Fredericksburg. Alarmed, he set out for Virginia, making his way right up to the front lines while the battle still went on. Brother George was not seriously hurt, but there were many badly wounded young men behind the lines with no one to care for them. Walt stayed to help. On December 28th, he accompanied a train-

load of wounded to a hospital in Washington, doing
what he could to relieve the misery of the journey.

The hospital was already full and badly under-
staffed. By now Whitman was involved in the lives of
the young men. He rented an inexpensive room near
the hospital, found part-time work, and served as a
volunteer in the hospital. He ran errands, often
buying needed little items for the soldiers out of his
own pocket. He wrote letters home for them. He
changed dressings on wounds and sometimes assis-
ted with amputations. He sat by the dying:

> *From all the rest I single out you, having a
>   message for you,*
> *You are to die—let others tell you what they
>   please, I cannot prevaricate,*
> *I am exact and merciless, but I love you—
>   there is no escape for you....*
>
> *I sit quietly by, I remain faithful,*
> *I am more than nurse, more than parent or
>   neighbor,...*
>
> *The sun bursts through in unlooked-for
>   directions,*
> *Strong thoughts fill you and confidence, you
>   smile,*
> *You forget you are sick, as I forget you are
>   sick,*

You do not see the medicines, you do not
  mind the weeping friends, I am with you,
I exclude others from you, there is nothing
  to be commiserated,
I do not commiserate, I congratulate you.[10]

Sometimes as he walked the streets of Washington going home from the hospital, he silently passed the President. So far as we know, they never met. A great love for Lincoln grew in Whitman. He was in the city that fatal night of April 14, 1865:

When lilacs last in the dooryard bloom'd,
And the great star early droop'd in the western
  sky in the night,
I mourn'd, and yet shall mourn with ever-
  returning spring.

Ever-returning spring, trinity sure to me you
  bring,
Lilac blooming perennial and drooping star
  in the west,
And thought of him I love....

In the dooryard fronting an old farm-house near
  the white-wash'd palings,
Stands the lilac-bush tall-growing with heart-
  shaped leaves of rich green,
With many a pointed blossom rising delicate,
  With the perfume strong I love,
With every leaf a miracle—and from this bush
  in the dooryard,

With delicate-color'd blossoms and heart-
*   shaped leaves of rich green,*
A sprig with its flower I break....
Here, coffin that slowly passes,
I give you my sprig of lilac.[11]

And so the child went forth, to the dooryard where the lilacs bloomed, to the shore where the mocking-bird cried for its mate, to the streets and the ferries of Brooklyn, to the battlefields of the Civil War where the young men died in agony, to the hearts and minds of people for stretching cycles of years, giving voice to their longing and their grief:

It avails not, time nor place—distance avails not,
I am with you, you men and women of a genera-
*   tion, or ever so many generations hence,....*[12]

But I also know that the child never left the house his father built. I have heard his laughter in the kitchen as he helps his mother; I have heard his sturdy little feet climbing the stairs to the second floor, and I know his promise:

I stop somewhere waiting for you.

"Out of the cradle endlessly rocking" the children go forth, generation after generation. They go forth to play, to school, to find work, to establish new homes where more cradles will rock and in the end they go forth from this world. And how soon the memory of their lives, often even of their names, is forgotten by the succeeding children in the endlessly rocking cradle.

I think of those who preceded me, and looking back along one line of my inheritance, I can go back only as far as my great-grandfather, whose name happened to be Adam. Even my father knew very little about this man, his grandfather. He was born in 1812, somewhere in Bavaria; he was a custom shoe-maker by trade, said to have been very skilled. In the midst of a severe depression in 1845, he and a group of relatives and neighbors went forth from Germany in a sailing vessel, seeking a better life in the new world. Eventually they settled in a little German-speaking town in northern Ohio, where he opened a shoemaking shop. He died a dozen years before my father was born.

My grandfather, Adam's son, came forth into the world before that long journey to America was over. He was born on the sailing vessel as it lay in quarantine in the New York City harbor, while the immi-grants were being cleared for entry into their new country. He grew up in the little town in Ohio, attended the one-room school, learned his father's trade, and avidly followed events in his country. He was very much anti-slavery in his feelings, and he gave his young heart to Abraham Lincoln.

When war broke out in 1861, he ran away from home, lied about his age, and enlisted in the Union army. He was wounded and spent some months in a hospital. Did Walt Whitman stop by *his* bed? I do not know, nor did my father. He carried a permanent disability, and after being discharged from the hospital, he returned home a hero, settled down to work with his father in the shop, and married a girl from North Germany who lived on a farm nearby.

My father was the fourth and last child to occupy the endlessly rocking cradle in that family. He was the darling of the family, the child on whom the sun shone, for was there not an omen in his birth? He came forth into the world on February 12, the birthday of the man his father most admired. Naturally my father grew up to be an amateur Lincoln scholar.

When he completed what education was to be had in the little town, the family agreed that he must go on. So he went forth to Toledo, where his elder brother lived, and attended high school there. Then his brother lent him the money to take a short course in typing at the Toledo Business College, and then additional money to buy a typewriter. Armed with a marketable skill and the tool of his trade, he went forth to a small Methodist college for more education. There he met my mother. He became a teacher, and later a school administrator.

He loved poetry, and he had a capacious memory for it. The poetry I absorbed from him in childhood is a precious inheritance, a lifelong joy, illuminating my days and the long wakeful hours of the night. And he loved Whitman. Early in life he taught me to recite *O Captain, My Captain* with appropriate fervor. Much of *When Lilacs Last in the Dooryard Bloomed* was familiar to me as I grew up.

My grandmother lived her last years with us, and she and I shared a room in the small apartment where we lived. She was badly crippled with arthritis and when she woke she would ask me to call someone to help her out of bed into her wheelchair. I remember the day she did not call, or move, and I cried out in panic for someone to come. My father came running. He stood quietly by the bed a moment, and spoke words I found strangely comforting to carry with me through that chaotic day:

> *Come lovely and soothing death,*
> *Undulate round the world, serenely arriving,*
> *   arriving,*

In the day, in the night, to all, to each,
Sooner or later delicate death. [13]

On a day when no visitors came to Walt Whitman's birthplace, I sat reading and musing. An even earlier memory suddenly came to me out of the mists of my early childhood. The year I was three, when "the lilac scent was in the air and fifth month grass was growing," the little sister died of whooping cough. I suddenly remembered standing quietly in the shadows of the dining room, half afraid, half curious, looking into the living room at the tiny casket, in the bay window. As I stood there, hidden in shadow, my father came in from the yard, with something in his hand. He stood looking down at the casket, and spoke words, portentous, full of mystery, that had lain buried in my memory all those years:

I give you my sprig of lilac...

So Walt Whitman was a guest of my life, out of the cradle. So he helped me shape my response to life and to death, and gave words to

The unknown want, the destiny of me...

Whitman's gift to me is his way of looking at life and death, a view that is at once rational and comforting. Robert Ingersoll, an unbeliever, speaking at

Whitman's funeral said that millions of people would hold him by the hand as they faced death, clinging to his large and hopeful vision. I find that this is so, for myself, and for others who are moved to speak of it. Death has lost some of its fearfulness because of his beautiful and brave words.

I do not know whether human personality survives physical death. I am content to wait and see what comes after death, open to any possibility. If it should turn out to be eternal sleep, that too is a gift after a full life.

But I know that we live in the lives of those we touch. I have felt in me the living presence of many I have loved and who have loved me. I experience my daughter's presence within me daily. And I know that this is not limited to those we know in the flesh, for many of the guests of my life shared neither time nor space with me.

And this I know also: Whitman's view of death as the eternal recycling of life is confirmed by modern physicists. The atoms and the molecules that come together for a time to make up living entities were all in existence from the beginning of our world. They come together, and then, sooner or later, they return to the earth to grow again in other forms, to be part of the continuing life of the planet.

Life, then, is a gift of time. For each of us the days are numbered. I am grateful for each day I have to walk this beautiful earth. And I do not fear the return to the earth, for I know, like Whitman, that it is part of myself:

> *I bequeath myself to the dirt to grow from the grass I love,*
> *If you want me again look for me under your boot-soles.*

> *You will hardly know who I am or what I mean,*
> *But I shall be good health to you nevertheless,*
> *And filter and fibre your blood.*[14]

We scattered our daughter's ashes in a garden in Chicago. Each year when the lilacs bloomed, we had a special sense of her presence.

But the lilacs also bloom perennially in Huntington, New York, in our day, as in Walt Whitman's time.

> *Failing to fetch me at first keep encouraged,*
> *Missing me one place search another,*
> *I stop somewhere waiting for you.*[15]

ENDNOTES

CHAPTER I

1. For the evolution of the writer's theological point of view, see Elizabeth G. Watson, *This I Know Experimentally,* available from Friends General Conference, 1520-B Race Street, Philadelphia, Pa. 19102. $1.50.
2. *The Complete Poems of Emily Dickinson,* Edited by Thomas H. Johnson, Boston: Little, Brown and Company. No. 49, p. 27.
3. *ibid.,* No. 943, p. 442.
4. *Emily Dickinson Selected Letters,* Edited by Thomas H. Johnson. Cambridge: Harvard University Press, 1971. No. 868, p. 293-4. First published in *The Life and Letters of Emily Dickinson by Martha Dickinson Bianchi.* Boston: Houghton Mifflin Co., 1924.
5. *Selected Letters, op. cit.,* from No. 268, p. 175.
6. *ibid.,* from No. 93, p. 89.
7. *Complete Poems, op. cit.,* No. 657, p. 327.
8. *ibid.,* No. 633, p. 313.
9. *ibid.,* No. 378, p. 180.
10. *ibid.,* No. 789, p. 384-385.

CHAPTER II

1. *The Complete Poems of Emily Dickinson, op. cit.,* No. 419, p. 200.
2. Rainer Maria Rilke, *Later Poems,* translated by J.B. Leishman. London: The Hogarth Press Ltd.
3. Rilke, *Duino Elegies,* The German Text, with an English translation, introduction and commentary by J.B. Leishman and Stephen Spender. New York: W.W. Norton and Company Inc. 1939. First Elegy, lines 13-14, p. 21.
4. Kaufmann, Walter, editor and translator, *Twenty German Poets.* New York: Modern Library, 1962. "From the Correspon-

dence with Erika Mitterer," p. 241. Also in *Twenty-Five German Poets: A Bilingual Collection,* edited, translated and introduced by Walter Kaufmann. New York: W.W. Norton and Company, 1975.

5. Rainer Maria Rilke, *Selected Poems,* with English translations by C.F. MacIntyre, Berkeley and Los Angeles: University of California Press, 1966, p. 1-2.

6. *Duino Elegies, op. cit.,* Commentary on the Fourth Elegy, p. 100.

7. Rainer Maria Rilke, *Poems 1906-1926,* translated with an Introduction by J.B. Leishman. London: The Hogarth Press, 1966. p. 213-214.

8. *Selected Poems, op. cit.,* p. 65.

9. *ibid.,* p. 45.

10. *ibid.,* p. 5.

11. *Duino Elegies, op. cit.,* First Elegy, lines 1-2, p. 21.

12. *Letters of Rainer Maria Rilke,* Vol. Two, 1910-1926, translated by Jane Bannard Greene and M.D. Herter Norton. New York: W.W. Norton and Co., Inc. 1947, 1948. Letter 60, p. 115.

13. *ibid.,* p. 117.

14. *Poems 1906-1926, op. cit.,* p. 193.

15. *Duino Elegies, op. cit.,* First Elegy, lines 79-84, p. 25.

16. Rainer Maria Rilke, *Selected Works, Volume II, Poetry,* translated by J.B. Leishman. New York: New Directions Publishing Corp., 1967, p. 204.

17. Rainer Maria Rilke, *Poems from The Book of Hours,* translated by Babette Deutsch. New York: New Directions Publishing Corp., 1941, p. 11.

18. *ibid.,* p. 31.

19. *ibid.,* p. 35.

20. *ibid.,* p. 13.

21. *ibid.,* p. 23.

22. *Twenty German Poets, op. cit.*

23. *Selected Poems,* translated by MacIntyre, *op. cit.,* p. 21.

CHAPTER III

1. Rilke, *Duino Elegies, op. cit.,* First Elegy, lines 65-67, p. 25.

2. *The Journal of Katherine Mansfield,* edited by J. Middleton Murry. New York: Alfred A. Knopf, 1933, p. 6.

3. Katherine Mansfield, *Poems*. New York: Alfred A. Knopf, 1931, p. 28.
4. *The Journal of Katherine Mansfield, op. cit.*, p. 38-39.
5. *ibid.*, p. 166-168.
6. *ibid.*, p. 135.
7. *ibid.*, p. xi.
8. *ibid.*, p. 196-197.
9. *ibid.*, p. 46.
10. *ibid.*, p. 65-66.
11. *ibid.*, p. 223.
12. *ibid.*, p. 254.
13. Olgivanna (Mrs. Frank Lloyd Wright), "The Last Days of Katherine Mansfield," *The Bookman,* March 1931, p.'6ff.
14. *Journal of Katherine Mansfield, op. cit.*, p. 255-256.
15. *ibid.*, p. 255.
16. Rilke *Duino Elegies, op. cit.*, First elegy, lines 85, 87-89. p. 25, 27.

CHAPTER IV

1. *The Journal of Katherine Mansfield, op. cit.*, p. 227.
2. Rabindranath Tagore, *Gitanjali*. New York: The Macmillan Company, 1934. No. 7, p. 6.
3. Rabindranath Tagore, *Fireflies*. New York: The Macmillan Company, 1928. p. 15.
4. *Gitanjali, op. cit.*, No. 87, p. 80.
5. Rabindranath Tagore, *The Gardener,* No. 61. *Collected Poems and Plays,* New York: The Macmillan Company, 1952. p. 128-129.
6. *Gitanjali, op. cit.*, xiii-xiv, xvi-xvii.
7. *ibid.*, No. 67, p. 62-63.
8. *ibid.*, No. 22, p. 18.
9. Rabindranath Tagore, *Stray Birds* XCV. *Collected Poems and Plays, op. cit.*, p. 299.
10. Elizabeth Gray Vining, *The World in Tune*. New York: Harper and Brothers Publishers, in association with Pendle Hill, 1954. p. 68.
11. *Gitanjali, op. cit.*, No. 93, p. 85-86.
12. *ibid.*, No. 90, p. 83.
13. *ibid.*, No. 1, p. 1.

14. Rabindranath Tagore, *Lover's Gift* and *Crossing*. London: Macmillan and Co. Limited, 1921. *Crossing* No. 75, p. 113-114.

CHAPTER V

1. Tagore, *Gitanjali, op. cit.,* No. 35, p. 27-28.
2. Alan Paton, *Instrument of Thy Peace.* New York: The Seabury Press, 1968, p. 90.
3. Alan Paton, *For You Departed.* New York: Charles Scribner's Sons, 1969. p. 88.
4. Alan Paton, *Cry, The Beloved Country.* New York: Charles Scribner's Sons, 1948. p. 79.
5. *ibid.,* p. 52.
6. *For You Departed, op. cit.,* p. 89.
7. *Instrument of Thy Peace, op. cit.,* p. 89-90.
8. *For You Departed, op. cit.,* p. 133.
9. *ibid.,* p. 156.

CHAPTER VI

1. Walt Whitman, *There Was a Child Went Forth,* lines 19-23.
2. *ibid.,* lines 24-25.
3. *ibid.,* lines 1-6.
4. *ibid.,* line 38.
5. Whitman, *Out of the Cradle Endlessly Rocking,* lines 25-31.
6. *ibid.,* lines 150-157.
7. *There Was a Child Went Forth,* lines 30-32.
8. Whitman, *Song of Myself,* lines 4-5, 91-95.
9. *ibid.,* lines 123-130.
10. Whitman, *To One Shortly to Die.,* lines 1-3, 6-7, 10-15.
11. Whitman, *When Lilacs Last in the Dooryard Bloom'd,* lines 1-6, 12-17, 44-45.
12. Whitman, *Crossing Brooklyn Ferry,* lines 20-21.
13. *When Lilacs Last in the Dooryard Bloom'd,* lines 135-138.
14. *Song of Myself,* lines 1339-1343.
15. *ibid.,* lines 1344-1346.

ABOUT THE AUTHOR

Elizabeth Watson grew up in Cleveland, Ohio, and graduated from Miami University, Oxford, Ohio with majors in Greek and English literature. She wanted to enter the ministry and spent two years studying theology at Chicago Theological Seminary and the University of Chicago Divinity School. Midway in the course she found 57th Street Friends Meeting, and came to feel that she was being called into the Religious Society of Friends for a non-professional ministry embracing all of life. For many years she worked in Chicago with a concern for race relations, the long-time job being with a community organization in a changing neighborhood. In 1972 the Watsons moved to Long Island, where George accepted the call to be Moderator (President) of Friends World College at Huntington. Since that time Elizabeth has been a free lance writer and speaker, and a curator of Walt Whitman's birthplace, a New York Historic Site in Huntington. The Watsons had four children, and four foster children, three of whom are sisters from Germany. They now have twelve grandchildren.